MW00465473

RICHARD COEKIN
EPHESIANS
FOR YOU

thegoodbook
COMPANY

Ephesians For You

© Richard Coekin/The Good Book Company, 2015. Reprinted 2017.

Published by:
The Good Book Company

Tel (US): 866 244 2165
Tel (UK): 0333 123 0880
Email (US): info@thegoodbook.com
Email (UK): info@thegoodbook.co.uk

Websites:

North America: www.thegoodbook.com
UK: www.thegoodbook.co.uk
Australia: www.thegoodbook.com.au
New Zealand: www.thegoodbook.co.nz

Unless indicated, all Scripture references are taken from the HOLY BIBLE, NEW INTERNATIONAL VERSION. Copyright © 2011 Biblica, Inc.™ Used by permission.

(Hardcover) ISBN: 9781910307656
(Paperback) ISBN: 9781910307649

Design by André Parker

Printed in India

CONTENTS

SERIES PREFACE

Each volume of the *God's Word For You* series takes you to the heart of a book of the Bible, and applies its truths to your heart.

The central aim of each title is to be:

- Bible centred
- Christ glorifying
- Relevantly applied
- Easily readable

You can use *Ephesians For You:*

To read. You can simply read from cover to cover, as a book that explains and explores the themes, encouragements and challenges of this part of Scripture.

To feed. You can work through this book as part of your own personal regular devotions, or use it alongside a sermon or Bible-study series at your church. Each chapter is divided into two shorter sections, with questions for reflection at the end of each.

To lead. You can use this as a resource to help you teach God's word to others, both in small-group and whole-church settings. You'll find tricky verses or concepts explained using ordinary language, and helpful themes and illustrations along with suggested applications.

These books are not commentaries. They assume no understanding of the original Bible languages, nor a high level of biblical knowledge. Verse references are marked in **bold** so that you can refer to them easily. Any words that are used rarely or differently in everyday language outside the church are marked in grey when they first appear, and are explained in a glossary toward the back. There, you'll also find details of resources you can use alongside this one, in both personal and church life.

Our prayer is that as you read, you'll be struck not by the contents of this book, but by the book it's helping you open up; and that you'll praise not the author of this book, but the One he is pointing you to.

Carl Laferton, Series Editor

To my beautiful daughters, Charlotte, Rhiân and Annabel, who each bring me more joy than they can possibly understand.

"The joy of the L<small>ORD</small> is your strength"
(Nehemiah 8:10)

Bible translations used:

- NIV: New International Version, 2011 translation (this is the version being quoted unless otherwise stated)

- NIV84: New International Version, 1984 translation

- ESV: English Standard Version

INTRODUCTION TO EPHESIANS

Ephesians is a spectacular **epistle**. Both times that I've preached through it over the last decade, it has profoundly reformed and united our church under God, and especially rekindled our reverence for Christ. I am not surprised that the great theologian, **John Calvin**, treasured it above all others. *Ephesians for You* has no other agenda than to introduce you to what Paul teaches in this biblical masterpiece.

Ephesians is packed with stunning passages, every chapter yielding fresh treasures. The epic explosion of praise for our blessings in Christ (Ephesians 1:1-14) deepens our appreciation of God's almighty rule; the celebration of God's amazing grace in raising us from death to life in Christ (2:1-10) humbles and moves us to worship him; the mind-blowing dimensions of the love of Christ (3:14-19) provides us with a new sense of security in him; the church-growth strategy of Bible teachers preparing all God's people for ministry (4:1-16) can mobilise our whole churches; the glorious description of marriage (5:22-33) will get us excited about heaven; and the climactic call to stand firm in Jesus' "armour" of gospel convictions (6:10-20) will clarify any confusion about spiritual warfare. Digging up these spiritual treasures will not only enrich your life but increase your confidence in sharing them with others.

Such glorious passages have proved ideal for private devotions and group discussions as part of our church's discipleship programme, just as much as for public preaching. Properly understood, this epistle is God's spiritual remedy to radically improve the spiritual health of your church and every ministry within it.

Paul's own Introduction

Ephesians begins with the author introducing his own letter:

"Paul, an apostle of Christ Jesus by the will of God,
To God's holy people in Ephesus, the faithful in Christ Jesus:

> Grace and peace to you from God our Father and the Lord
> Jesus Christ." (**1:1-2***)

The author identifies himself as the **apostle**[†] Paul. The evidence points to the great missionary and church-planting apostle writing this letter from prison, probably in Rome, in about AD 61-62. He describes himself as "an apostle of Christ Jesus", emphasising that he writes as one of Christ's authorised and empowered witnesses to proclaim the eternal and cosmic will of God, which we will find set out in Ephesians.

Paul addresses his letter to "God's holy people in Ephesus, the faithful in Christ Jesus" (**v 1**). The earliest manuscripts don't include the name of Ephesus. Since the letter is general in style, without any reference to local people or issues, it seems likely this was a circular letter written for all the churches in the region (now western Turkey), which had been planted from Ephesus, where Paul had been senior pastor for 2½ years.

We know from Acts 19 that Ephesus was cosmopolitan and commercial: a **pagan** city devoted to the temple of the Greek goddess Artemis. This would explain the great emphasis in this letter on Christ's supremacy over the devil and demonic powers. Paul calls his readers: "the faithful in Christ Jesus" (Ephesians **1:1**), because this letter especially celebrates the blessings of living together "in Christ", by faith in him.

Paul wishes them "grace and peace" (**v 2**)—combining both customary Gentile and Jewish greetings—because these will be massively important themes in this letter. He will celebrate God's "grace" as his undeserved kindness and the origin of all our blessings in Christ (eg: 1:6; 2:7). And "peace" is the summary of all the blessings resulting from being reconciled to God and to each other in Christ (eg: 2:14, 15, 17). If grace is the *origin* of God's plan to gather us into the blessings of his church in Christ, then peace is the *result* of it which demonstrates in the spiritual realms the triumphant wisdom of the gospel of Christ crucified.

---

* All Ephesians verse references being looked at in each chapter are in **bold**.
[†] Words in **grey** are defined in the Glossary (page 213).

The Structure and Message of Ephesians

The letter neatly divides into two halves of three chapters each (for a fuller outline, see the Appendix). Chapters 1 – 3 focus on gospel doctrine. They proclaim God's cosmic plan to unite everything under Christ (chapter 1), by reconciling us to God and each other by his death and resurrection (chapter 2), through the proclamation of the revealed mystery of the gospel of Christ crucified for all nations, which is displayed in the spiritual realms in the church (chapter 3).

Then chapters 4 – 6 focus on church practice. They call us to respond by preserving our unity under Christ. This is done by continuing to gather people under Christ by preparing each other for ministry, growing in maturity, and speaking the truth in love (chapter 4) in order to be made new in our minds and living distinctive Christ-honouring lives in the church, in the home and at work (chapter 5). The climactic finale of the letter calls readers to stand firm in the armour God has given them in the gospel against the lies of Satan, which threaten to divide us from God and each other; and to keep on praying in the Spirit for world mission—which is victory in spiritual warfare in our churches (chapter 6).

There are five distinctive emphases and phrases in Ephesians that reflect Paul's message:

1. The problem of sin and judgment, and its remedy in Christ, are not like in Romans, presented as unrighteousness deserving wrath and needing **justification** through faith in Christ. Rather, in Ephesians "sin" means to be spiritually dead in a slavery that alienates us from God and excludes us from his people—for which the remedy is reconciliation to God and his people in Christ.

2. The gospel is presented as the "mystery" of God, previously hidden but now revealed, through which people of all nations can be reconciled to God and included in the new humanity in Christ.

3. The "heavenly realms" are the spiritual and eternal dimensions in which Christ has already been resurrected and enthroned in glory

over Satan and all his powers—the realm in which the church now displays the triumphant wisdom of God in the gospel of Christ crucified, as people from all nations gather under the word of Christ, standing firm against the lies of the devil, protected by the armour of gospel convictions.

4. "Church" is far more important to God than just a useful vehicle for collecting disciples. Each local church is an earthly expression of the heavenly gathering which is his personal inheritance; the body, building and bride of which his Son is the head, corner-stone and husband; the trophy cabinet of his saving grace; and the demonstration of the triumphant wisdom of the cross to his enemies in the heavenly realms.

5. All our blessings are "in Christ"; he is not only the means of our blessing, but the One we live in, for we are united by faith to him and share in his resurrection victory over Satan, sin and death.

The mind-blowingly encouraging central message of Ephesians is this: God's eternal cosmic plan is to "bring unity to all things in heaven and on earth under Christ" (1:10), who is already raised in triumph to rule over all evil powers for the safety of his church. This church is reconciled to God and each other through his death and resurrection; and the "mystery of the gospel" (6:19) is that people of all nations can share in the marvellous blessings of Christ so that, "now, through the church, the manifold wisdom of God should be made known to the rulers and authorities in the heavenly realms" (3:10), as the trophy cabinet of his saving grace. So in learning to be made new in our thinking to live as children of light in the world, we will be protected from the assaults of the devil's lies by standing firm in the convictions of the gospel, as we keep on praying and evangelising the world.

However ordinary we may feel, every local church that works to-gether to teach the gospel of Christ is proclaiming the victory of his death and resurrection in the spiritual realms. Your church matters enormously to God—and so Ephesians is definitely for *you*!

1. EVERY BLESSING

In this glorious passage, the apostle Paul launches an avalanche of praise for God. In the original Greek, it's one long, breathless sentence. He begins by summarising what he's so excited about: "Praise be to the God and Father of our Lord Jesus Christ, who has blessed us" (**1:3**). Even though Paul is chained up in prison (6:20), he feels incredibly blessed—and he wants his Christian readers, then and now, to realise how incredibly privileged we are as well. He summons the praise of our hearts towards God, because God deserves it—and because articulating our blessings helps us to enjoy them all the more.

Where are these Blessings?

The privileges that provide such comfort and reassurance to a believer, even in the midst of trials and troubles, are found "in the heavenly realms" (literally "heavenlies"—**1:3**). This is a crucial phrase that Paul repeats five times in Ephesians, and which we need to grasp if we are to understand the letter.

The heavenly realms are the spiritual dimension in which God and all spiritual powers are dwelling. They are not just heaven (for evil powers exist in the heavenly realms, but not in heaven), and not earth (for this is not a matter of flesh and blood), and not the future (for we wrestle with our spiritual enemies in the heavenly realms now—6:12). The "heavenly realms" means *the spiritual dimension*:

(a) where we have already been blessed (**1:3**)

(b) where Jesus has been enthroned for ever over all evil powers (v 20)

(c) where we have already been raised to be seated with Christ (2:6)

(d) where the victory of Christ over evil powers at the cross is spiritually demonstrated in one church gathering under Christ, displayed in the unity of our earthly church gatherings under his word (3:10)

(e) where we need to stand firm against the spiritual assaults of the evil powers by praying for the fearless proclamation of the gospel to all nations (6:10-20).

Put simply, we are blessed in the "heavenly realms" through sharing in the resurrection of Christ!

The blessings Paul is speaking about are not the trivial and temporary trinkets of wealth and property, or even of him being released from prison, but the eternal treasures of personal reconciliation with God which we experience in this spiritual dimension. They belong to all Christians from the time we first trust in Christ. And although we can't enjoy them as fully now as we shall one day enjoy them in glory, they fill our hearts with joy even now.

The stunning word here is "every" (**1:3**). Each believer has received in Christ every possible spiritual blessing from God. None are being withheld. Christians will have different gifts and different ministries and different circumstances, but we all possess every spiritual blessing in Christ. We can safely ignore anyone offering us their special way to extra blessings, because we already have them all in Christ. And we need never feel less blessed or more blessed than another believer. God has given each Christian everything to enjoy in eternity.

But what are "spiritual blessings"? They are benefits that the Holy Spirit applies to our experience of knowing God in the spiritual dimension. So, although we must take up our cross to follow Jesus, ready to suffer for the salvation of others (Mark 8:34), we are always at the same time experiencing the blessings of sharing in the resurrection of Christ, and looking forward to an extravagant abundance of joy in arriving home to be with him in the renewed creation.

How do we access such blessings? Very simply, they are found completely and only "in Christ" (Ephesians **1:3**). Eleven times in this marvellous sentence that runs from **verse 3** to **verse 14**, we're reminded of all we have "in Christ" (or "in him" or "through him" or "under him") by faith in him (**v 3, 4, 5, 6, 7, 9, 10, 11, 12** and twice in **v 13**). God wants us to remember that we owe everything to his Son. We're blessed not just "through" Christ, as the mechanism for getting blessed, but personally "in" Christ, to whom we are united by faith. These are his fabulous resurrection blessings, and we enjoy them if we have turned to trust in him.

If we have a friend who owns an exciting sports car, although we can admire it from a distance, we only really enjoy it when we are racing along the motorway in the car with them. In the same way, Christ shares his privileges with those who are with him—like a driver with his passengers, a commander with his troops, or a husband with his wife. We've been blessed with all spiritual blessings in the heavenly realms "in" him. And all we will have to do to finally experience them fully is… die. Even I can manage that!

Well, what would you think are the greatest blessings of being a Christian? We can summarise the apostle Paul's sensational top three blessings under the following headings:

1. Being chosen for adoption by the Father (**v 4-6**)

2. Being redeemed for unity by the Son (**v 7-10**)

3. Being sealed for inheritance by the Spirit (**v 11-14**)

Surprised by his top three? I guess we will never be as excited as he is until we properly understand them. So let's unwrap these presents and find out why these are such fabulous blessings.

Chosen by God

Long before we ever chose to follow Jesus, God the Father "chose us" (**v 4**)! This is called the "election" of believers or the "predestination" (**v 5**) of our futures. Many Christians find this hard to understand. Some think it's cruel. Why on earth would Paul think this was our top spiritual blessing?

Yet the great nineteenth-century preacher Charles Spurgeon wrote: "Election sets the soul on fire with enthusiastic delight in God". And, like all the great **Reformed theologians** and theological statements, the **Anglican 39 Articles of Faith** declare: "The godly consideration of predestination and our election in Christ is full of sweet, pleasant and unspeakable comfort to godly persons." Are you surprised?

Most importantly, Jesus himself plainly taught election and predestination as part of the good news of the gospel—for instance: "All those the Father gives me will come to me, and whoever comes to me I will never drive away" (John 6:37). He's saying that no one can be saved unless the Father has chosen to give them to Jesus.

It's helpful to realise that God's election of sinners for salvation is simply the exercise of God's universal **sovereignty** in our human arena, because he is the one "who works out everything in conformity with the purpose of his will" (Ephesians **1:11**). Indeed, whenever we pray, we are acknowledging that God is in control. And whenever we pray for God to save someone, we're unconsciously recognising that God, with his sovereign control, must elect people for salvation if they are ever to be saved. We instinctively understand that sinners cannot become Christians unless God chooses to save them. But we may struggle with the idea that God chooses some and not others for salvation for at least three reasons. God choosing people can seem to:

- undermine **evangelism** ("God will certainly save his elect, so there's no need for us to bother too much with telling people about Jesus")

- undermine humility ("We're superior—because we're the chosen ones")

- undermine holiness ("We don't need to strive to please God because once saved, always saved").

These are serious and understandable concerns. But Paul's careful explanation of election here gently answers each of these anxieties.

First, being chosen by God shouldn't diminish the importance of evangelism because: "He chose us in him" (**v 4**), and how do sinners come to him? "You also were included in Christ when you heard the message of truth, the gospel" (**v 13**). It is through the preaching of the gospel of Christ that God calls his elect into Christ. God uses our evangelism to save his elect. Indeed, if God hadn't elected anyone for us to call through the gospel, there would be no point in us trying to evangelise sinners, because they're spiritually dead (2:1). But since God has elected many, we evangelise everyone, in the confidence that he can involve us in reaching his elect!

So election is actually a great motivation *for* evangelism! It's what we hear in Jesus' encouragement to Paul to keep preaching the gospel in Corinth "because I have many people in this city" (Acts 18:10). Churches should pray confidently and then evangelise urgently,

> Evangelism is the joyful privilege of finding God's elect with God's gospel.

precisely because God has chosen many for salvation "in Christ". If he hadn't done so, our evangelism would be pointless. Since he has chosen many, our evangelism is the joyful privilege of finding his elect with his gospel, like miners digging for gold in a pit.

Second, being chosen by God shouldn't diminish our humility because we were chosen "before the creation of the world" (Ephesians **1:4**). We're not saved because we turned out to be cleverer or more deserving than other people. The decision was made long before we were even born—before God even created the world. Being "chosen" should humble us by reminding us that we're not more deserving than our atheist or Muslim friends. If we had chosen God without him first choosing us, then we could be proud of our wisdom. Since he first chose us, we should only ever be humble—our salvation was entirely his gracious initiative.

Third, our election shouldn't diminish our enthusiasm for holiness, because we were chosen "to be holy and blameless in his sight" (**v 4**). Far from undermining holiness, we've been chosen to be accepted by God as holy and blameless on the basis of the holy and blameless life lived for us by Jesus. And then, in gratitude for being saved, we're called to gradually become holy and blameless like him. Because we've been chosen to play for the highly privileged "Holy and Blameless Team", captained by Jesus, we will want to become holy and blameless like him. Election is a reason to be holy! Especially when you hear what we're chosen for...

Chosen for Adoption

"In love he predestined us for adoption to sonship through Jesus Christ" (**v 4-5**). Sinners are not naturally God's children. But with incredibly generous love, God has chosen us in Christ for rebirth and adoption into God's family. Despite how unlovely we are, in the great torrent of affection he has poured out upon us, God has not just predestined us to become his servants, but his sons! He has chosen to unite us with his Son by faith to enjoy his Son's privileges.

We therefore enjoy the tender love of our heavenly Father, carefully providing our daily needs, pardoning our sins, protecting us from unhelpful harm, disciplining us in the way we should go, and showering us with undeserved kindnesses. We enjoy our heavenly Father's constant attention to our prayers, for he's never sleepy or forgetful, never grumpy or uninterested, never powerless to help or unsure of what to do. Indeed, in Christ we are brought right into the family of the **triune** God himself, able to whisper in the ear of our Father!

Moreover, as adopted sons, we enjoy the comfort of God's global people gathered in church families. We will generally find that when we cry out in distress, he doesn't remove us from our suffering, but brings brothers and sisters from our church family into our troubles, to carry us when we're too weak to stand up ourselves.

And as adopted sons, we share in the inheritance of the Son. So we shall each receive a glorious inheritance that can never perish, spoil or fade, in the Son's eternal kingdom. This is why Paul describes all Christians—women and men—as "sons". In the Old Testament, it was the firstborn sons of Israel who inherited land, because God was teaching us about our faith, which shares in the glorious inheritance of his own firstborn Son, who would inherit everything (Psalm 2). So by faith in God's Son, men and women alike are adopted by the Father to share in Jesus' inheritance. (Indeed this was familiar to Paul's Gentile readers because in the first-century Greco-Roman world, slaves in childless households were sometimes adopted to inherit the family estate.) What an incredible privilege it is for us now to be chosen for adoption by God the Father to inherit a share of his Son's glorious estate in heaven! The great theologian J.I. Packer writes:

> "You sum up the whole of New Testament religion if you describe it as the knowledge of God as one's holy Father. If you want to judge how well a person understands Christianity, find out how much [they make] of the thought of being God's child and having God as [their] Father." (*Knowing God*, page 224)

The Spiritual Solar System

We often find election hard to swallow because we don't really think that those who aren't chosen will deserve God's judgment (which usually reveals that we don't really think that we deserve judgment either). But understanding that we have been chosen for adoption turns our world upside down in a wonderful way. It's a spiritual "Copernican revolution".

Nicholas Copernicus was the sixteenth-century astronomer who discovered that the sun doesn't rotate around the earth, but that our planet rotates around the sun. The sun is the centre of the solar system, and not our world. Likewise, as sinners we like to think that God and the world rotate around us. We arrogantly question whether to allow God to have any part in our world and our future. But election turns this worldview completely upside down; it recognises that we are hell-deserving sinners, and so the question is whether God could choose to allow us any part in his world in his future!

As we struggle to get our minds around God's sovereign electing grace, it's helpful to think of becoming a Christian as being like walking through a narrow door (this illustration is based on one in Harry Ironside, *In the Heavenlies: Ephesians,* pages 27-28). On the front of the door is painted the words of Jesus' gracious universal invitation: "Come to me, all you who are weary and burdened, and I will give you rest" (Matthew 11:28). When we walk through the door and look back at it from the inside, we read the comforting reassurance of his sovereign election: "In love he predestined us for adoption" (Ephesians **1:4-5**).

When we arrive in heaven, God will welcome us, and we can imagine him saying: *I am so glad to welcome you into my home at last—for I chose to save you for my Son before I made the world; I sent my Son to die for you on the cross; I arranged history to ensure your birth and steer your life; I brought someone to explain the gospel to you and opened your eyes to recognise Jesus as your Saviour and Lord; I carried you when you were weak and held on to you when you tried to run away; and now, finally, I can welcome you into my home. It is so good to see you—I've loved you for such a very long time!*

Here is the mind-blowing top blessing of faith in Christ: we have been chosen for adoption by the Father.

Questions for reflection

1. "God has given each Christian everything to enjoy in eternity." How does this excite and comfort you today?

2. Did you relate to any of the concerns raised regarding predestination on page 14? How did the answers to them help you think of God's election as good news?

3. Re-read the penultimate paragraph on this page. Meditate on what God has done for you and how he sees you if you are "in Christ". How does it make you feel?

PART TWO

Redeemed

In the Bible, "redemption" means liberation from slavery upon the payment of a ransom. This was familiar in Roman society in the redemption of slaves, but the biblical background is in Exodus, when the Israelites were slaves in Egypt. They were liberated from captivity under Pharaoh, and from God's judgment upon their sin, by the blood of sacrificed "Passover" lambs. This is the background to Paul's second great spiritual blessing in Christ: "In him we have redemption through his blood" (**v 7**).

In 2:1-3, we will see Paul describing the natural condition of sinners as enslaved in following "the ways of this world" (captive within our sinful culture), "the ruler of the kingdom of the air" (Satan inflames our sin with his lies), and "the cravings of our flesh" (our compulsive sinful appetites). We were all once enslaved like this, unable to break free... but Christians have been redeemed—liberated from the miserable captivity in which we once languished. We are now free to think outside the box of worldly culture with the ideas of God in Scripture. We are freed from the deceptive lies of Satan with the liberating truth of God. We are free to resist the temptations of our flesh by the power of the Holy Spirit. We're free to become the people we were created to be, made in the image of Christ. And although we often wander back into the filthiness of our cells to sin like slaves, the door of the cell has been permanently opened by Jesus, who patiently keeps walking us out into the light again.

But how is such freedom possible?

Exodus recounts how the Passover lambs were sacrificed in the place of the Israelite firstborn sons, suffering the punishment that Israel deserved (the death of all their firstborn), and the lambs' blood was then painted over the doorposts of Israelite houses. When God saw that the death penalty for sin had already occurred, his judgment "passed over" the Israelites. It is similar now for Christians. We trust in the precious blood of Jesus, who was sacrificed in our place for our sins on the cross. We are protected by the blood of our "Passover" sacrifice, Jesus (1 Corinthians 5:7). God has been fully satisfied that the death penalty we deserve for our dreadful sins has been fully suffered by himself in Christ on the cross. For God to allow such a sacrifice for our sins is grace. For God to *provide* such a sacrifice for our sins is amazing grace. For God to *become* such a sacrifice for our sins is grace beyond our comprehension! But what will such redemption mean in practice?

Primarily, this means we have "the forgiveness of sins" (Ephesians **1:7**). As the Israelites were freed by the Passover lambs from captivity to Pharaoh under the judgment of God, so we have been redeemed by Christ's sacrifice from captivity to guilt under God's law, which once gave Satan his power to demand our punishment in hell. All our sins of thought, word, deed and neglect—whether past, present or future—have been completely pardoned. This is not because God doesn't care how dreadfully we've treated him and other people. It's because Christ has suffered the punishment we deserve for them all. If you have ever experienced a frightening debt being paid off by a sacrificially generous parent or friend, you've tasted a droplet of the joy of having your sins forgiven in Christ.

Why would God do such a magnificent thing, when we have treated him with such contempt? It's not because of anything in us, but because of something sensational in him. It's all happened "in accordance with the riches of God's grace that he lavished on us ... with all wisdom and understanding" (**v 7-8**). God redeemed us only because he is abundantly wealthy in grace, his undeserved kindness. Grace is not a kind of strength we receive through the **sacraments** of the church to live better lives. God's grace is his costly gift to us in Christ. It is well summarised as GRACE—God's Riches At Christ's Expense.

What does this mean today?

First, it means we enjoy freedom from fear. If we trust in Christ as our Passover sacrifice, we don't have to fear that Satan will point out our sins to God and successfully demand that we are punished, either in this life or beyond death, for our debts have been fully satisfied with Christ's blood.

Second, it means we enjoy freedom from guilt. We don't have to constantly feel like a wretched disappointment to God—desperately trying to impress him and other people—since all our sins are now pardoned and the record of our sins has been permanently deleted. God is now completely satisfied and pleased with us, because of Christ's perfect life, which was completed for us when he died.

But we are not only redeemed *from* punishment, but *for* something wonderful.

Redeemed for Unity

The Ephesians had been brought up in the fear of the Greek **occult** mystery religions but, as Paul will explain more fully in chapter 3, the "mystery" (secret) of what God is doing in the world had now been made clear by Christ to his apostles, and proclaimed by Paul (3:3). As Paul puts it here, God has "made known to us the mystery of his will according to his good pleasure, which he purposed in Christ" (**1:9**). This revelation is a massive privilege. God grants us the extraordinary privilege of knowing his eternal plans because we are friends of his Son (John 15:15)!

God and his plans are always beyond our complete understanding, but there's no longer any mystery—the secret has now been revealed. This is a challenge because there is now no excuse for ignoring God since he has revealed himself and his plans in Christ. But this is also a

> God grants us the extraordinary privilege of knowing his eternal plans.

huge relief because God has revealed his eternal plans, not just in the short term, but for eternity, "when the times reach their fulfilment"

(Ephesians **1:10**). We now know what his intentions are for us and our world. So what is this great plan?

God's awesome plan is "to bring unity to all things in heaven and on earth under Christ" (**v 10**). His plan is to bring together (literally, to "sum up") everything under Christ, including rebellious evil spirits in the heavenly realms and rebellious human beings on the earth. Everything will be re-ordered in appropriate submission to God. This is not undermining Jesus' clear and frightening teaching that after death, unrepentant sinners and demons will be condemned to hell (eg: Matthew 25:41). Paul is simply explaining that God's just order will be fully restored everywhere, under the rule of Christ. The divine Architect has published his glorious construction plan, and, having laid the sure foundation in the death and resurrection of Christ, the completion of his glorious new creation is now just a matter of time.

The purpose of God redeeming us (spiritually now, and one day bodily with all creation, Romans 8:21-23) is the "summing up" of all things under Christ. The focus of the plan is not us, but Christ. The goal was not just redeeming us but also uniting us under the rule of Christ. The best thing about this plan is not the unity, but the unity under Christ. There have been many Caesars, emperors, popes, führers and corporate CEOs who planned to unite the world under their global domination. Thankfully, all have failed, for their rule was tyrannical and foolish. By contrast, since Christ is compassionate and wise, to be united under his rule will bring us contented happiness in the splendid heavenly garden-city-church governed by him.

> The focus of God's plan is not us, but Christ.

This means that we now have confidence for the future. Contrary to the speculations of "**Open Theologians**", he has not left any part of his plan uncertain or risky. All that happens will always happen "in conformity with the purpose of his will". It's precisely because our

God has planned everything and has everything under control that Christians can relax and not worry about the things we don't know and can't control. There is a certain and glorious future awaiting believers, even as we struggle now with personal failures and addictions, or debilitating physical and mental conditions, or miserable jobs or unemployment, or painful singleness, loveless marriages, divorce or widowhood. Whatever we face, Christians can be sure that already and for ever we will live in unity under Christ.

Sealed

The top blessings in Christ are to be *chosen for adoption by the Father*, *redeemed for unity by the Son*, and now thirdly, *sealed for inheritance by the Spirit*.

Paul celebrates the inclusion of his Gentile readers in God's cosmic reconciliation plan: "And you also were included in Christ when you heard the message of truth, the gospel of your salvation" (Ephesians **1:13**). He then celebrates the security of their salvation by explaining some wonderful dimensions to the work of God the Holy Spirit, who indwells every believer from whenever we begin to place our faith for salvation in Christ: "When you believed, you were marked in him with a seal, the promised Holy Spirit, who is a deposit guaranteeing our inheritance until the redemption of those who are God's possession" (**v 13**).

A "seal" was a mark of ownership and protection, which in Roman culture was often branded upon cattle or slaves. God's seal of permanent ownership and constant protection of his people is the Holy Spirit of God himself. He is therefore like the birthmark of all God's children. It is as though we have all been marked with a spiritual UV marker pen, visible in the heavenly realms, marking us out as those belonging to God, completely safe from all frightening powers.

Moreover, says Paul, the Holy Spirit is the "deposit"—the "first instalment"—of eternal life, guaranteeing the "full payment" of enjoying God in heaven, because he is God within us. He is like the delicious first course of the sumptuous spiritual feast to come, in the new creation. Remembering this will enable us to avoid two common errors. First, we'll avoid thinking that our joy in the presence of God is only for the future. We can already enjoy something of heaven now in a personal intimacy with God that is enabled by his Spirit. But second, we'll avoid thinking that our current experience is all there is, when it is actually only the deposit—a taste of what is yet to come! The Holy Spirit's ministry in us now is a mouthwatering foretaste of the feast we shall enjoy in the presence of God.

Since the Holy Spirit is the "deposit" or first instalment of life with God, his presence is "guaranteeing" our full "inheritance" in the kingdom of God. Having sacrificed his Son to purchase us from hell for heaven, the Father will not fail to ensure that we arrive safely in heaven, through the indwelling of his powerful Spirit, who will maintain our faith in Christ until we arrive home.

The wonderful assurance of salvation for anyone who believes the gospel (that Jesus is Christ our Lord, who came as our King, died for our sins, rose to rule and will return to judge) is the irreversible election of the Father, the irreversible redemption of the Son and the irreversible indwelling of the Holy Spirit. Our glorious future could not be more secure!

Two Phrases, Four Times

Having celebrated these spectacular three blessings of being chosen for adoption, redeemed for unity and sealed for inheritance, we finally need to appreciate two magnificent phrases that each appear four times in this torrent of praise. They tell us how to respond to all that we have seen.

First, Paul emphasises that these blessings have been granted *according to his will* (**v 1, 5, 9, 11**). He wants his readers to rejoice that God is accomplishing his grand plan! The history of the world is not random. We're not accidents, and our lives are not pointless. Everything is being executed by God exactly according to his will and purpose, so there's no need to be anxious when things go wrong. Like a complex tapestry, the side of life that we experience often seems like a shapeless tangle of loose ends. But from the other side of the tapestry, which God sees, everything is working out beautifully, precisely according to plan.

Moreover, Paul emphasises that God's blessings in our lives are intended to be "to the praise of his glory" (**v 14**, and also **v 3, 6, 12**). These wonderful privileges are meant to stir our hearts to serve him with the worship of our whole lives, and to open our mouths to praise him in adoration and evangelism. When we're feeling sorry for ourselves, or going through difficult times, or being persecuted for our faith in Christ, we can return to this glorious passage to be reminded of how extravagantly blessed we are in knowing Christ.

Indeed, this glorious passage is worth learning so that we never forget. We are not merely to grit our teeth. We're consciously to revel in God's gracious blessings of election for adoption by the Father, redemption for unity by the Son and sealing for inheritance by the Spirit—to appreciate the exquisite joy of being saved and to live to the praise of his glory. For whether we are riding on the highest peaks of joy and success or sinking in the lowest troughs of pain and failure, Christians can always sing: "Praise be to the God and Father of our Lord Jesus Christ, who has blessed us in the heavenly realms with every spiritual blessing in Christ"!

Questions for reflection

1. What difference does knowing where everything is heading in the future make to us as believers today, do you think?

2. How do the words "sealed" and "deposit" help you to appreciate the work of God's Spirit in you?

3. How could you praise God for both a "peak", and in a "trough" you've recently experienced, or are experiencing right now?

2. PRAYING FOR OTHERS

In another extraordinary passage, Paul reveals to the Ephesian churches what he's been praying for them. As in most of his letters, he's providing warm reassurance of his affection for them and explaining what he thinks they most need from God. But when we compare the content of his prayer with our own praying, we'll probably be astonished by how seriously theological it is! It doesn't contain any requests for material blessings like better health or jobs; or for relational blessings at work, or for marriages or in raising children. It's a prayer for deep spiritual blessings in knowing God. As we explore Paul's prayer points, we'll be learning a lot about how to pray.

What is Prayer?

Prayer just means speaking to God. God speaks to us through the words of Scripture, and we respond to him in the words of prayer. The Bible celebrates prayer as an amazing privilege shared by the adopted children of God with the Son of God. Our heavenly Father always listens, gives us peace when we pray, and will always do what is best for us to become like Jesus (1 John 5:14-15; Philippians 4:7; Romans 8:28).

Our prayers are like breathing. So when our praying is neglected, we soon become spiritually sick. While he was imprisoned for his faith in Bedford, England, John Bunyan (the celebrated author of *The Pilgrim's Progress*) wrote a wonderful little book now published as

Praying with the Spirit and with Understanding Also (first published in 1662). In it he brilliantly describes healthy prayer as:

"a sincere, sensible [fervent], affectionate pouring out of the heart or soul to God, through Christ, in the strength and assistance of the Spirit, for such things as God has promised, or according to his Word, for the good of the church, with submission in faith to the will of God."

That is the kind of prayer we find here and elsewhere in Paul's letters.

Notice that he begins: "For this reason..." (**v 15**), meaning: *Because of what I've just said in verses 1-14 about God gathering his chosen, redeemed and sealed people together under Christ...* Paul continues: "Ever since I heard about your faith in the Lord Jesus and your love for all God's people"—Paul recognises, in the reports of these Christians' distinctive lifestyle, that they bear telltale cross-shaped birthmark of God's true children. They have the "vertical" dimension of faith in the Lord Jesus, which trusts in his sacrificial ministry on the cross (rather than in our own ministry in the church). And they have the "horizontal" dimension of love for all God's people, whatever their ethnic or social background (and not just for those like themselves or for those who could be beneficial). Real Christians always demonstrate growth in both of these dimensions: faith in Christ and love for all believers.

So, because Paul is convinced that these Ephesians are clearly "in Christ", and therefore blessed with all the wonderful privileges described in verses 1-14, he has "not stopped giving thanks for [them]" (**v 16**). Immediately, the apostle is setting us an example for our own prayers. Paul prayed unceasingly—not just sporadically, but regularly; generously—not just selfishly but for other people; and gratefully—appreciating God's work in their lives and church, and not just in his own. How encouraging and humbling it must have been for the Ephesians to discover that this great apostle of Christ, usually ferociously busy and now suffering in prison, constantly made time to thank God for them! It poses a challenge to us: will we pray like this for other people?

We don't need to worry that if we pray less for ourselves, we or our church might be neglected, for Jesus said that our heavenly Father always knows what we need (Luke 12:30). Prayer isn't about providing for ourselves or our church, like taking cash from a cash machine. It's about maintaining our relationship with our heavenly Father. He'll always provide fully for us and for our churches, but he wants us to learn to care more about our brothers and sisters than ourselves. This is why the Lord's Prayer is a plural prayer: "*Our* Father ... Give *us* today *our* daily bread ... forgive *us our* debts as *we* also have forgiven *our* debtors ... lead *us* not into temptation, but deliver *us*" (Matthew 6:9-13).

Having revealed that he prays for his readers with thanksgiving, Paul now begins to describe his prayers of request for them, in the light of God's great plan to unite all things in heaven and on earth under Christ, to parade his victory over Satan in the spiritual dimensions (Ephesians 1:10). When we learn that prayer is not about getting God to accomplish our plans, but about gladly submitting ourselves to his, we will find that when we turn his plans into our prayers, they are constantly being answered! Many Christians struggle without this emphasis. If God "does not lie or change his mind" (1 Samuel 15:29), and if he "knows what you need before you ask him" (Matthew 6:8), then what is the point of praying at all? But prayer is not about getting God to submit to my will, but about submitting ourselves to his.

The great **Reformer** John Calvin clarified six great biblical reasons why we should pray:

1. to learn to depend upon our heavenly Father

2. to purify the desires of our hearts

3. to be content with whatever he provides

4. to appreciate more deeply his generous faithfulness

5. to enjoy without guilt the many gifts he provides; and...

6. to trust him to constantly provide our daily needs.

Calvin summarised such biblical prayer as "digging up the treasures" promised to us in Scripture. And it will become our happy experience that God often delays giving us the things he has planned to give us until we ask for them in prayer, so that we realise that he is looking after us, because he loves us.

Imagine two young men who leave school to train as apprentice-managers in a paper mill. One is the adopted son of the general manager and the other is the son's friend from school. When they start work, the general manager hands them both the company business plan to read, and warmly invites them both to come and talk to him at any time. "Come and chat about what we're doing whenever you want—my door is always open to you," he says.

At first, both young apprentices regularly pop up to the general manager's office, but gradually the friend becomes disillusioned and stops bothering. The son asks his friend: "Why don't you visit Dad's office anymore?" "There's no point," says the friend: "He ignores all my suggestions, and every time I ask him for more holiday he says 'no'! I suppose he does whatever you want, because he's your dad!" "Oh no," declares the son: "I don't ask him to do what I want! I'm new here, but he's been running this business for ever—he knows what he's doing! And I don't ask for more time off, because I know he mustn't treat me differently from the other workers!" "So why do you keep going up to his office?" asks the friend. The son replies: "Well, I ask for help to do my job, and I want him to know that he has my support—and I suppose I just like being with him!" The friend replies sullenly: "That's because you're his son and one day you'll run the business with him". "Yes, perhaps you're right," smiles the son.

> We don't pray to get God to fit into our plans, but to give ourselves to fit into his.

As sons and heirs of our heavenly Father, we don't pray to get God to fit into our plans, but to give ourselves to fit into his! So what should adopted children of the General Manager pray for each other? Paul says he asks the Father to give them deeper knowledge of three things they already have in Christ: to know God better (Ephesians **1:17**), to know the hope to which he has called them (**v 18**), and to know the incomparably great power he has committed to getting them there (**v 19**).

To Know God Better

First and before all else, Paul prays for his Christian friends in Ephesus: "that the God of our Lord Jesus Christ, the glorious Father, may give you the Spirit of wisdom and revelation, so that you may know him better" (**v 17**). Paul's primary desire for them is very simple: it is that they will *know God better.*

Why? Because God is so unutterably captivating in his gracious holiness that knowing him will be our supreme blessing for eternity. It's striking that Paul reports his prayers for this "knowledge" of God in each of his prison letters (to the Ephesians, Colossians, Philippians and to Philemon) but nowhere else! This may be partly because of the false teachers in the region who were promoting their ecstatic visionary experiences of "knowing God" (Colossians 2:18-19), but probably also because knowing God becomes especially precious when you are experiencing persecution, as Paul was.

The greatest blessing that anyone can experience is to know God, and to know him better every day. Paul wrote: "I consider everything a loss because of the surpassing worth of knowing Christ Jesus my Lord, for whose sake I have lost all things" (Philippians 3:8). C.H. Spurgeon once preached a sermon, "The Immutability of God", in which he said:

"Nothing will so enlarge the intellect, nothing so magnify the whole soul of man, as a devout, earnest, continued investigation of the great subject of the Deity. And while humbling and expanding, this subject is eminently consolatory [comforting]. Oh, there is, in contemplating Christ, a balm for every wound; in musing on the Father, there is a quietus for every grief; and in the influence of the Holy Spirit, there is a balsam [treatment] for every sore. Would you lose your sorrow? Would you drown your cares? Then go, plunge yourself in the Godhead's deepest sea; be lost in his immensity; and you shall come forth as from a couch [bed] of rest, refreshed and reinvigorated. I know nothing which can so comfort the soul; so calm the swelling billows [waves] of sorrow and grief; so speak peace to the winds of trial, as a devout musing upon the subject of God."

How desperately sad, then, that we can acquire so much knowledge in our professional life and can have so many close friends we know well, and yet settle for knowing God only superficially! Whatever else we pray for other Christians, let us make sure we pray that they (and we) may know God better.

So Paul asks "the God of our Lord Jesus Christ, the glorious Father"—since in his human nature, Jesus lived for his Father as a human being should live for God—for "the Spirit of wisdom and revelation" (Ephesians **1:17**). He isn't suggesting that the Holy Spirit would ever leave his Christian readers. He is simply praying that, of the many ministries with which the Holy Spirit could bless them, he would particularly bless them with a wise understanding of God, as he is revealed in Christ in his word.

In the Old Testament, the Holy Spirit is called the "Spirit of wisdom" (Isaiah 11:2), but calling him the Spirit of "revelation" is quite new. Paul probably introduces this term to emphasise the new and exciting revelation in the gospel of the previously hidden "mystery", which he will elaborate in chapter 3. This stunning revelation is that whatever our personal and cultural background, anyone can be reconciled to God and to each other through the death of Christ, as part of God's eternal plan to unite everything under Christ in the church. There's no suggestion here that the "Spirit of wisdom and revelation" will bring revelations from God outside Scripture, but rather, a deeper understanding of God as he is revealed within Scripture, so that "you may know him better" (Ephesians **1:17**). Through the ministry of God's

Spirit speaking through the living words of Scripture, we actually get to know God himself! It's our supreme privilege as Christians, not just to know *about* him, but to know *him* personally!

We can get very excited about knowing famous people in our celebrity-driven culture. My youngest daughter was recently grinning from ear to ear for days after spending an afternoon with Paul Hollywood, star of the hit TV programme *The Great British Bake Off*. But far more exciting than meeting celebrities is knowing the supreme Being, our Creator and Saviour God, through Christ in Scripture. Of course, knowing God is far more than intellectual (though not less)—it is an informed, relational delight in him.

> As Christians, we don't just know *about* God; we know *him*, personally.

Knowing someone well who loves you is a deeply satisfying joy. My wife, Sian, and I recently celebrated 25 years of marriage with a romantic trip to Rome. But when I think about it, the best thing about the last 25 years, and the thing I look forward to in the next 25 years, is not the places we may visit, but getting to know her better—because, despite the inevitable road bumps in every marriage, she remains captivating to me. And human marriage is but a dull picture of the marvellous relationship all Christians can enjoy—the intimate joy of knowing almighty God as our heavenly Father! He really is incomparably captivating. So let us pray for each other, for our families and our church families, to get to know God better! For as J.I. Packer puts it:

"We are cruel to ourselves if we try to live in this world without knowing about the God whose world it is and who runs it. The world becomes a strange, mad, painful place, and life in it a disappointing and unpleasant business, for those who do not know God. Disregard the study of God, and you sentence yourself to stumble and blunder through life blindfold, as it were, with no sense of direction and no understanding of what surrounds you. This way you can waste your life and lose your soul … Our aim in studying the Godhead must be to know God himself better. Our concern must be to enlarge our acquaintance, not simply with the doctrine of God's attributes, but with the living God whose attributes they are." (*Knowing God*, pages 17, 21)

So in our prayers in church, at the end of our small-group studies and church meetings, with our flat-mates or our children or our spouse, before we go to sleep, commuting on the train in the morning or on the bus in the evening, let us pray for each other—not just to be happy, but to know God better. For in the glories of his being and his works, God is the source of the deepest satisfaction and joy to his adopted children.

Questions for reflection

1. How does the list of reasons to pray on page 29 motivate your own prayer life? Were there any on that list which you had not thought about before?

2. "We don't pray to get God to fit into our plans, but to give our-selves to fit into his." Is this truth reflected in how often you pray, and what you pray? How does it need to shape your prayers?

3. Who could you commit to praying for each day for the next year, that they would know God better and find him more and more to be their deepest satisfaction and joy?

PART TWO

To Know Greater Hope

After praying that his readers will know the living God better, Paul asks "that the eyes of [their] heart[s] may be enlightened" (**v 18**). He knows that the way we "see" in this world—what we value and desire or fear and avoid—is not just a rational decision based upon information neutrally observed. Our perspectives depend upon our values, which are shaped by the affections of our heart.

The word "heart" is used in the Bible not to describe the organ pumping blood around our limbs, but the centre of our physical and spiritual being, combining our intellectual understanding and our personal affections. So Paul prays that the "eyes of [their] heart[s]" will be enlightened by God to love the things that God loves, so that these Christians will see the world the way God does, which is the way it really is.

It is vital to understand that so often in our Christian lives, God doesn't want to alter the circumstances of our lives, but to alter the way we see those circumstances, by changing our hearts. For example, the apostle is suffering in prison, but we don't hear him asking for prayer to be released, but for courage to "make known the mystery of the gospel, for which I am an ambassador in chains" (6:19-20). Those around him who do not know God or understand the gospel might see him as a defeated preacher, trapped in the misery of a Roman dungeon. But with the eyes of his heart enlightened by the eternal plans of God, Paul sees himself as a dignified ambassador of Christ, gathering others under the rule of Christ, with a wonderful opportunity to **evangelise** his fellow prisoners and guards, and so to demonstrate in the heavenly realms that Christ is enthroned in victory over his enemies. That is quite a shift of perspective!

We need to learn to pray for each other that the "eyes" of our hearts—the way we view the world we live in—will be enlightened by God's Spirit through God's word, with such deep affection for God and the truths of his gospel that our situation completely changes. A filthy and depressing prison is recognised as a glorious stage for an evangelistic drama in the theatre of the heavenly realms! Setbacks become opportunities to trust in Christ enthroned on high; cruel persecutions are no longer pointless suffering, but wounds received in the battle for supremacy that has been decisively won at the cross by our King, who will soon return to reward his loyal soldiers.

I wonder if the apostle had in mind here the wonderful example of Caleb, one of the Israelite spies sent into the promised land of Canaan to assess the opposition Israel would face in receiving their inheritance. Caleb trusted the LORD when everyone but **Joshua** doubted God's gospel promise to give them the land. Why? Because: "I brought [**Moses**] back a report according to my convictions"—literally "according to my heart" (Joshua 14:7).

Can you see what Caleb was doing? He wasn't just being optimistic about their chances, despite the power of their enemies. And he wasn't just being braver than the other spies by being willing to have a go. He saw the same land as the other spies, but in the light of the truth of who God is and what God had promised. Caleb trusted that nothing and no one could prevent the LORD from keeping his promise to bring his people into their inheritance. We are to pray for that same faith of Caleb for each other. To pray for gospel convictions in our hearts that makes us trust in the power and goodness of God to keep his gospel promise to give us our inheritance in heaven, despite the satanic enemies of God and the many problems we face.

> Being a Christian is essentially about living a life of uniquely confident hope.

When we see life in this way, Paul says, we will then "know the hope to which he has called you" (Ephesians **1:18**). In the gospel, God has "called" and summoned us to the invisible but completely certain future that the Bible describes in different places as our hope, eternal life, an incorruptible righteousness, a new creation, heaven, and God's glory—the kingdom of the risen Christ. Being a Christian is essentially about living a life of confident hope that is unique in this world. In Western culture today, there is generally lots of misdirected faith, and lots of superficial love, but no realistic hope for the future. This is why so many in our generation are escaping from the reality of the future that is hurtling towards them by hiding in alcohol, or work, or sexual excitement, or entertainment, or devotion to their family. But Paul prays that his readers will know, with a confidence that shapes their ambitions and daydreams, this hope of "the riches of his glorious inheritance in his holy people" (**v 18**).

Inheritance

We might think that Paul wants to tell his readers about what we will inherit from God, of how happy we'll be in heaven. But it's the opposite! Paul wants his readers to grasp the "riches" (**v 18**)—the extravagantly abundant wealth of the glorious inheritance that God has prepared for himself to enjoy in eternity—in... us! Isn't that staggering? God Almighty, who could have provided anything he wanted for his enjoyment in eternity, has chosen to enjoy forever with saved and **sanctified** sinners like us! It's utterly mind-blowing—he's chosen, redeemed, adopted, and sealed sinful wretches like us as his children, to become the bride for his beloved Son! And his plan is to bring us all "on vacation" into the glories of his eternal "rest"—to enjoy our company and shower us with abundant blessings for ever as his inheritance!

I recognise a little of this joy. I am at an age when my children are leaving home for university and jobs, and sometimes bring their girlfriends and boyfriends home for dinner or to go on holiday with us. I really enjoy welcoming these lovely young people into our lives and showing them some hospitality. But I don't think my hospitality could extend to welcoming anyone who had hurt or hated my children. Yet God's love is so extraordinarily merciful and generous that he has invited people like you and me, who were once the enemies of his beloved Son, to spend eternity with Jesus in paradise! That is breathtaking forgiveness and incredible hospitality. Most Christians tend to assume that we'll sneak in the back door of heaven, hopefully with no one noticing, and then hide in the shadows of the back row of the heavenly stadium. But with astonishing generosity, God has planned that we will be *his inheritance* for ever.

However hard your life currently is, can your heart see how magnificent this will be? It's impossible to illustrate this wonderful future—but let me try. One of the reasons I love going to my in-laws is the overwhelming sense when we walk in the door that they have massively looked forward to us being there. So much has been carefully planned. Vast amounts of food have been cooked, expensive wines have been opened and lined up on a dresser ready for the meal, and gifts of baked cakes and jars of marmalade have been prepared for us to take home. It's lovely to feel so welcome. Unbelievably, God has been preparing for our arrival for eternity past, because we are his glorious inheritance!

But how will we get there? We're all going to die and, while our spirits go to be with the Lord Jesus in the place of the dead, our bodies will either be cremated and our ashes scattered, or will slowly decompose in a grave and be dispersed in the soil or sea or wherever we die. I don't want to be overly morbid, but how on earth will our spirits ever be reunited with our disintegrated bodies and become fit for heaven? We need to know the third glorious thing that Paul prays for his friends to know...

To Know His Power

Paul prays that the Ephesians will grasp how secure their future is—that is, that they will grasp God's "incomparably great power for us who believe" (**v 19**).

We know that God has incomparably great power; just look at the galaxies he made to decorate our "ceiling"! The shock here is that the

Creator's incomparable power is being exercised for "us who believe". All his awesome power will be made available to accomplish his amazing plan to bring us together under Christ in heaven for ever. Paul offers his readers three reassurances that our hope is justified:

First, it is reassuring to realise that God's power to raise us has already been demonstrated in raising Christ, for "that power is the same as the mighty strength he exerted when he raised Christ from the dead and seated him at his right hand in the heavenly realms" (**v 19-20**). Since it is Christ our representative King who was raised, we belong with him (indeed, in terms of spiritual reality, all his people are already there—2:6). Christ's victorious resurrection guarantees our resurrection and our place in heaven is secured. We could say that God has practised resurrecting us in raising Jesus. He's done it before, so we know he can do it again.

> God has done resurrection before, so we know he can do it again.

But what about the evil spirits—Satan and his demons—who will try to accuse us under God's law and drag us down to hell, and who are so much more powerful than us?

Paul prays that his readers will not be afraid, but realise that our hope is certain because of a second reassurance. Our resurrection is secured by Christ's **dominion**: "far above all rule and authority, power and dominion, and every name that is invoked, not only in the present age but also in the one to come" (**1:21**). Our Saviour is enthroned far above all the satanic powers and magical demons of which Ephesian culture was so fearful—indeed, far above every name and position imaginable. So no one can get remotely close to taking us away from our Saviour. Indeed, incredible though it sounds, God has "placed all things under his feet and appointed him to be head over everything *for the church*" (**v 22**—my italics). Christ is the "head", directing and protecting his body, the church, both in heaven and in every local expression of it on earth. Christ is governing this world for the benefit of the church in becoming more like him, and for being with him. Even the persecution he allows is only for the purification and reward of his church.

And why does Christ care so much for the church? Because of Paul's third reassurance: the church is "his body" (**v 23**). Christ is the head: ruling, steering, providing for, empowering and using his churches in the world. Christ, who fills the whole universe with his governing presence, makes the fullness of his divine power especially present in the church to bless us, in whom he demonstrates his victory over sin, Satan and death. So, however small and vulnerable his churches may look, every genuine church gathered through the gospel under the rule of Christ by his word enjoys "the fullness of him who fills everything in every way" (**v 23**). God is intensely present in each believer and in every church to bless us with his salvation, his holiness and his gifts, because each is incredibly precious to God. Christ, who died to save his body, now lives to serve his body. All God's resurrection power is being employed to gather churches together, and then keep churches trusting Christ until they physically arrive to join the great heavenly gathering around the throne of Christ. We shall most certainly be raised to life with him, because he himself was raised to life and we are his living body. Our head cannot be separated from his body!

Paul was in the habit of praying that the Ephesians would be strengthened by knowing that their hope of heaven was certain because God had already raised Christ our King to be supreme in the spiritual realms, because he is now sovereign far above all our enemies, and because God has appointed him King to ensure that he brings his people home to be with him for ever.

We need to learn from Paul how to pray for other believers in our family, in our church and across the world. Let's not just pray for them to know earthly peace and prosperity, health and happiness. Let us pray for them to experience the huge spiritual privileges—of *knowing God* better, of *knowing the hope to which he's called us*, and of *knowing the power which he has committed to bringing us home to be with him*. Next time we are tempted not to pray, or think we don't know what to pray for, we can employ these verses in confidence that this is the kind of prayer that others need and our heavenly Father loves to answer.

Let us pray.

Questions for reflection

1. Which Christians do you know who need you to pray for a deeper appreciation of the future hope they have in Christ?

2. Which Christians do you know who need you to pray for a deeper sense of God's power at work in and through them?

3. Paul not only prays for his Christian friends—he encourages them by telling them what he's praying for them. How will you do this with the people whom the two questions above have prompted you to pray for?

3. DEATH TO LIFE BY GRACE

Why do Christians get so excited about God's "grace"?

People write songs and books about his "Amazing Grace". They give their churches and even their children the name "Grace"! What is all the fuss about? God's "grace" means his generosity, his undeserved kindness towards us. But why is God's grace so "amazing"? This passage reveals all—it beautifully explains why God's grace is simply extraordinary and shows why it is worth celebrating for eternity.

Let's recall Paul's message to this point: he began with an explosion of praise in 1:3-14 for the blessings of the church in Christ (especially being chosen for adoption by God the Father, redeemed for unity under God the Son, and sealed for inheritance with God the Holy Spirit). In 1:15-23 he then revealed his prayers for his readers to be empowered by God's Spirit to know God better, know the hope to which God has called them, and know the resurrection power that God has committed to achieving his plans for them. Now in chapter 2, he explains and celebrates two aspects of peace and reconciliation which are necessary to bring us together under Christ: namely, reconciling us to God (**v 1-10**), and then reconciling us to each other (v 11-22).

So first, Paul must explain how Christians have been reconciled to God through Jesus. To summarise simply, he says we've been brought from death by nature... to life by grace. Buckle up— this is an exciting roller-coaster ride! We must begin with the dreadful condition we were in when Christ found us.

Spiritual Diagnosis

We all tend towards an inflated view of ourselves, like grimy miners down in a dark pit, comparing ourselves with each other and imagining ourselves relatively clean. So we find it hard to understand God's **wrath**, and therefore our need of a Saviour. The writer of Psalm 36 wisely observed: "I have a message from God in my heart concerning the sinfulness of the wicked: There is no fear of God before their eyes. In their own eyes they flatter themselves too much to detect or hate their sin" (Psalm 36:1-2).

So we need to honestly face the truth and take a good look at ourselves in the mirror of the Bible. Here, our human nature is painfully exposed but accurately diagnosed as being spiritually dead and captive under a triple tyranny:

a) the ways of the world

b) the influence of Satan, and...

c) the wickedness of our nature.

Without Christ we all deserved everlasting wrath. This diagnosis reveals not just how bad we really were, but how utterly helpless we were.

This examination of our inner being is truly alarming. But imagine three patients with heart disease being asked into the doctor's surgery after their scans and X-rays. "Well," said the doctor, "I do have some good news for you, but you won't realise what good news it is unless I first tell you the bad news... All of you have serious heart disease because you've been chain-smoking for over thirty years; and unless each of you has major surgery, you will all be dead within a year."

"Outrageous!" shrieked the first patient. "How could you criticise me like this! I came in here for some reassuring encouragement and you've made me feel terrible. It's a disgrace!" And he stormed out of the clinic.

The second patient responded with menacing fury: "How dare you! Who do you think you are telling me my heart needs surgery! I'll find many other doctors to tell me I'm fine—and I'm a lot healthier than some smokers I know. And I *feel* fine! You're the most arrogant doctor I've ever met." And he too stomped out of the clinic.

The third patient sat quietly for a moment. "Doctor," he said, "it's a terrible shock to hear I need surgery. But thank you for telling me the truth. I'm so relieved that there's good news of an operation to save me—please tell me about it."

It's like that here. Paul has wonderful news to share of God's grace. But we will never truly rejoice in it until we recognise how appalling our natural condition really is without Christ.

Paul begins with a summary diagnosis: "You were dead in your **transgressions** and sins" (Ephesians **2:1**). He isn't just saying that we faced physical death, or even eternal spiritual "death" in separation from God in hell. He means that we were all born spiritually dead to God, like spiritual lepers—utterly lifeless and insensitive to our Creator. We grew up understanding the intellectual concept of "God" and may have practised any number of religions, but we had no personal relationship with him. When people say that Western culture is becoming more spiritually hungry, it may be true that people are becoming more self-reflective, or becoming more religious, but it cannot mean that people are really moving towards God—because they're spiritually dead. Corpses don't get hungry and they can't move.

> People cannot move towards God because we're spiritually dead, and corpses can't move.

Paul explains that this deadness is evident in behaviour characterised "in" lives full of "transgressions". This means breaking God's laws (Exodus 20:1-17); for instance, when we break his first **commandment** by devoting our worship to his good gifts—like family, home, status and pleasure—instead of to him; or breaking his seventh commandment when we commit adultery in our minds; or breaking his ninth commandment when we bear false witness in gossip; or breaking his tenth commandment when we covet other people's bodies or possessions. Our "sins" are our failures to love God and other people.

Prison Guards

Sinners are held captive in this death and sin by three kinds of bondage—by a trinity of tyrants:

- ■ "the world"—an external cultural tyranny

- ■ "the devil"—a hostile supernatural tyranny

- ■ "the flesh"—an internal compulsive tyranny

They're like three prison guards ensuring that sinners cannot escape from spiritual death. Indeed, if you think this might be an overly pessimistic diagnosis, just see if you can break free from these compelling influences for one week without God's help (even Christians will never be completely free from these tyrannies until we're resurrected into the new creation, because our human nature remains until then— read Romans 7:7-25).

Let's consider each tyrant briefly, not because we enjoy wallowing in **masochistic** self-loathing, but because we'll never feel our urgent need of the Saviour, or appreciate God's grace in sending him, until we begin to realise how corrupt and helpless we were, and how dreadful the punishment we deserved was.

We were captive to "the ways of this world" (Ephesians **2:2**). This means the cultural worldview of our sinful race, of which there are two principal kinds at present across the globe (I am indebted to Tim Keller for the kernel of these ideas).

First, there is what we might call the "traditional" worldview of older generations and non-Western cultures, concerned with social **hierarchy**, family responsibility, duty, good works and evidence. The gospel of the Bible challenges this traditional view today, much as it challenged the Jewish religious outlook of the first century, with our condemnation under God's law and our humbling need of forgiveness and the gift of the righteous life we need to qualify for heaven, all found in Christ and him crucified.

Second, there is what we might call the "emergent" worldview of Western culture that is flooding younger generations of our world via the internet. This is the confident assertion of personal **autonomy**— claiming freedom to choose our own spiritual outlook and objects of worship. This worldview is profoundly narcissistic (self-loving) and conveniently pluralistic (choosing our own way to God). It resurrects the ancient idols of power and status, wealth and leisure, sex and pleasure, education and career, family and children, etc. as options for pleasing ourselves. Such objects of our worship will always consume enormous sacrificial effort from us but ultimately cannot satisfy or save us, because they're not God; so they will gradually foster cynicism about the authority and worth of any ultimate being, a cynicism which Satan inflames with the lies of **secular atheism**. The

> It is not only teenagers who are driven by their peer culture.

gospel challenges this emergent worldview—familiar in the Roman Empire of New Testament times—with the resurrection of Jesus from the dead to rule and return to judge idolatry.

David Wells helpfully observes:

"You can recognise 'the ways of this world' wherever sin seems acceptable and righteousness seems strange."

(*Losing our Virtue*, page 4)

Before God reveals himself to us in Christ through his word, we cannot break free from the worldview in which we're raised and educated. It's not only teenagers who are driven by their peer culture. In truth, we've all been captive to the ways of the world. We can't think outside this box any more than a jellyfish can think outside of the ocean. We were all held captive in "the ways of this world".

The Ruler of the Kingdom of the Air

The second tyrant holding us captive was "the ruler of the kingdom of the air", who is Satan (**v 2**). In Hebrew thinking, Satan exists in "the air"—the spiritual sphere between earth and heaven (the "heavenly realms" means the spiritual dimension of all three). Satan has worked in us all and remains active in every unbeliever, tempting them with lies to doubt the existence of God's word, the truth of God's word and the motives behind God's word.

Satan has been doing this ever since the Garden of Eden (Genesis 3:1-7). It is not that unbelievers are generally possessed by Satan or his demons (though some involved with witchcraft are), but that we were willingly persuaded by his lies because we were "disobedient" (Ephesians **2:2**)—that is, we wanted the lies of the devil to be true so that we could continue being sinful. We'll learn more about satanic powers in chapter 6, because Christ's victory over them is a primary reason for Paul writing this letter and is therefore the reassuring climax to it.

We need to recognise that our unbelieving relatives and friends remain gripped by this spiritual evil, from which only Christ can deliver them. We mustn't be naively shocked or bitterly vengeful when an aggressive colleague or religious extremist or government officer is hostile to lovely and law-abiding Christians. Remember that Satan inflames their sin. And we mustn't despair, for Christ has defeated Satan on the cross and risen to rule far over him, soon to return to punish him. Let's not be arrogant towards those still under his influence, for we were all once captive to his lies.

Captive to our Cravings

The third kind of human bondage is to "the cravings of our flesh" (**2:3**). This word "flesh" does not mean just our physical body but our whole human nature. These cravings include our desperate appetites for exploitative pornography or selfish luxury as well as our incurably self-indulgent attention-seeking and proud self-glorification.

We know that the "ways of this world", the influence of "the ruler of the kingdom of the air" (**v 2**) and "the cravings of our flesh" (**v 3**) really are an addictive triple bondage, because not only are we unable to break free of them, but we didn't want to change. As unbelievers, we generally enjoyed our sins, boasting about them around the office water cooler, drooling over magazine articles and TV programmes about them, and supporting laws that forbid any criticism of them.

Indeed, we defended ourselves from accusation or feelings of guilt by claiming that we couldn't help ourselves. We blamed our genetic make-up, our social upbringing or our financial circumstances. This passage confirms that our sin is very natural to us. We were all once captive in sin to our worldly culture, our satanic enemy and our fleshly cravings, and were guilty before God—and we liked it that way.

Children of Wrath

We were, therefore, "by nature deserving of wrath" (**v 3**) (literally "children of wrath"—God's punishment is our deserved inheritance). The wrath of God is not just an impersonal consequence, nor vindictive rage; but God's consistently pure anger towards evil, which means he will fairly punish sin. Paul is not describing any particularly degraded or decadent sector of our society, but all of us— for he says in **verse 3**: "All of us also lived among them". Although our genetic make-up, family upbringing and social circumstances determine precisely how we express our sinful nature, we all deserve to face his wrath. We must be careful not to allow our imagination to exaggerate God's word, as medieval artists once did, but we also need to remember that the biblical images and **metaphors** used in Scripture are describing a terrifying reality.

All humanity will spend eternity in the presence of God—his people will be flooded with his blessing; his enemies will be filled with the torment of his wrath. Jesus taught plainly that sinners in hell will exist in the shrivelled isolation of utter despair and loneliness, racked with sobbing and pain. Jesus used the horrific phrase: "where 'the worms that eat them do not die, and the fire is not quenched'" (Mark 9:48) to describe it. His image of worms forever gnawing at our insides like maggots in a corpse illustrates the inner anguish of being stricken with agonising regret; his image of living in flames illustrates life in the presence of a holy God, not because he is a torturer, but because God is as holy as a consuming fire. To exist in God's holiness unforgiven will be like living unprotected on the surface of the sun. (Some have suggested that biblical descriptions of hell should be placed in an order: exclusion, then punishment, then **annihilation**. But these are **concurrent** perspectives upon the same dreadful experience, as eternal as the joys of heaven—Matthew 25:46.) Yet, tragically, there's no indication that unbelievers in hell will ever want to stop sinning to live for God.

We find it impossible to imagine how we'll ever be able to rejoice in God's justice when loved ones are in hell. Perhaps—just as we rightly want vicious paedophiles and violent drug barons to be punished—when we finally recognise the true horror of sin and unrepentant hatred for God, we will marvel not at the horror of hell but at the blessing of heaven, more stunned by God's grace than his judgment.

We sometimes protest that a permanent hell seems too severe for one short life of sin. But the gravity of a crime is unrelated to its duration, for a momentary sin is often symptomatic of permanent wickedness. One cruel argument with a sister can be the leakage of a soul full of festering bitterness towards God and jealousy towards others, originating in obsessional self-love.

> Wickedness can be as much about inaction as action.

And wickedness can be as much about inaction as action. Imagine two newly-qualified school teachers, Matt and Tom, starting their first jobs and looking for cheap accommodation. To their delight, a family friend, a wealthy music mogul with a stunning estate near their school, offers them his mansion. "I'll be abroad for a few years on business," he says. "I don't really need money—so enjoy my mansion for £10 a month." The friends are ecstatic. "Just stay in touch," says the owner.

"It's a big place and will need looking after, so respond to my emails, pay the rent and have a fantastic time!"

The lads move in, each taking one wing of the mansion. Matt is a wild man—a party animal—and soon the east wing is trashed: cigarette burns on the furniture, beer stains on the walls and mud trodden into the carpets. Everyone knows that when the owner returns, Matt will rightly be kicked out.

But Tom is different—quiet and polite. He's so well-behaved that the west wing is spotless. Everyone assumes that the owner will be glad to let Tom stay.

But when the owner returns, he kicks them both out. Friends of Tom are shocked. But to anyone who asks, the owner explains: "Look, I realise they're different—Matt trashed the place while Tom was tidy. But they treated *me* exactly the same! Both of them utterly ignored me; neither bothered to answer my messages and the house is now seriously damaged; they couldn't even be bothered to pay the small rent I asked for. Since they've so abused my kindness, I'm afraid they can't stay." No one could quarrel with that! This story illustrates the different ways we treat God. We live in God's world, enjoying his extreme generosity. God expects us to listen to his messages in Scripture, look after his creation, and seek his help in prayer. But we ignore and disobey him. Some of us trash our lives—the relational wreckage is everywhere. Others of us are clean living, religious and well behaved. But we ignore him, proudly presuming that we belong in heaven. Some of us even ignore him for so long that we declare him dead and claim the house is now ours. What matters is how we treat God as we live in his world as his tenants.

It's no surprise that God will not allow us into his paradise. The tragedy is that we don't realise how dreadful life will be without his daily kindness.

Can you see how serious our natural condition was? These verses reveal the humbling truth that I am not naturally a good person. Without God I am spiritually dead, enslaved to worldly cultures, Satan's influence, and fleshly desires, and should now be facing an eternity of suffering in hell. We all desperately needed a saviour—we were dead by nature.

The good news comes next...

Questions for reflection

1. Look back on your life before you became a Christian. How were the three tyrants Paul identifies at work in you?

2. Have you ever really appreciated that, by nature, all that your abilities and achievements deserved was "wrath"? What difference does accepting this make to your view of God?

3. Why would an under-appreciation of the hard truths of verses 1-3 mean that we could never really rejoice in being saved by Christ?

PART TWO

But God...

Paul now jubilantly celebrates God's sacrificial and sovereign grace in reaching down to us in our utter helplessness. When we were beyond help and without hope, Paul says: "But ... God..." (Ephesians **2:4**). Our salvation was, is, and will always be entirely attributable to God's free intervention.

It is easy sometimes to think or behave as though God was obliged to save us. But he was under absolutely no obligation whatever to act... and yet he did! Four key Bible words in this passage celebrate the beauty of God's character revealed in sending his Son:

■ Love (**v 4**): God's commitment to bless us for ever in Christ.

■ Mercy (**v 4**): God withholding the punishment we deserve because Christ endured it for us on the cross.

■ Grace (**v 5, 7, 8**): God generously giving us what we need in the obedience of Christ even unto death.

■ Kindness (**v 7**): God's compassion in shrinking himself down to become one of us to exchange places with us on the cross!

So Paul explains the origin of our salvation: "Because of his great love for us..." (**v 4**). He will later pray that his readers will have power to grasp how great this love is: "How wide and long and high and deep is the love of Christ" (3:18)—wide in being accepting of people of every nation, culture and background; long in lasting eternally from before creation until after the Lord returns; high in exalting us to the right hand of the Father; and deep in giving his only beloved Son to suffer in our place.

Resurrection

Here in chapter 2, Paul continues: "God, who is rich in mercy..." (**v 4**), for God is fabulously wealthy—not just owning everything, but "rich in mercy", abounding in compassionate willingness to be our lightning conductor, unleashing the billion volts of the holy wrath that we deserve upon himself in Christ on the cross. However, Paul doesn't dwell for long upon the cross here, because his focus in Ephesians is less upon our guilt and need of justification, and more upon our alienation from God and need of reconciliation, accomplished on the cross and then secured in the resurrection of Christ. God's mercy is revealed in three stages of resurrection, with cosmic implications:

1. He "made us alive" (**v 5**)—through faith in Jesus, we share in his representative death and resurrection as our King. Therefore, the resurrecting power of his Spirit breathes out his word in re-generative power (John 3:5-6; 1 Peter 1:23). We're now like light bulbs plugged into the mains power of a light socket as Jesus electrifies us with his spiritual life.

   Ezekiel was given a dramatic illustration of this miracle in his vision of a valley of dry-bone skeletons (Ezekiel 37). This valley of death represented the spiritual condition of Israel, but we all live in that valley, in villages, towns and cities full of apparently healthy people who are really spiritual skeletons, utterly dead to God. Yet in Ezekiel's vision, the skeletons were brought to life by God's word and Spirit, becoming a vast army serving the Lord, just as Christians around the world have been regenerated by God's Spirit through God's gospel, brought to life in the living Christ. This isn't just resuscitation to life in this world, but resurrection to life in the kingdom of heaven...

2. He "raised us up" (Ephesians **2:6**)—in our representative King we've already been accepted into heaven when Jesus was raised. If Wayne Rooney scores a winning penalty for England, only one man kicks the ball, but all of England win the game! Likewise, when our captain, Jesus, died and rose, we died and rose with him. Since heaven is now our present dwelling, it must be our future destination. And we'll not merely be spectators...

3. He has "seated us with him in the heavenly realms" (**v 6**)—we're already seated with Jesus in his position of unique authority at the Father's right hand in the heavenly realms, in full view of the defeated satanic powers, who hate God and his people (1:20-21). Like places reserved at a wedding banquet in accordance with the groom's seating plan, seats are reserved for us by Jesus at his wedding feast. Since he has already sat down, it is as if we have sat down, because our places are secured by him! We shall soon take our seats to fulfil the destiny for which we were created, to be united with Jesus to rule the new creation, and the spiritual realms of which the Ephesians were so frightened.

But what does God hope to achieve by this incredibly costly plan? It is all so that "in the coming ages he might show the incomparable riches of his grace" (**2:7**). God wants to spend eternity showering us with blessings! Paul has already celebrated God's "glorious grace" (1:6), "the riches of God's grace that he lavished on us" (1:7-8), and now "the incomparable riches of his grace" (**2:7**). The purpose of God's great plan to bring everything together under Christ for the church is now revealed. It isn't just an exercise in tidying up the mess, or in putting down the rebellion. His plan is to forever pour out a torrent of kindness upon us in heaven, and demonstrate for ever in the spiritual dimension the wisdom of his grace revealed in the cross. Every day, we shall be flooded with fresh blessings of his grace to explore and to prompt us to praise our Saviour.

Past and Present

The contrast between our past condition of spiritual death and our current condition of living by grace in Christ (**v 4-7**) could not be more dramatic. Imagine yourself as a decaying corpse (we were spiritually dead), trussed up in chains inside a coffin (we were captive to the world, the devil and the flesh), heading inexorably into the flames of the crematorium fires (objects of God's wrath)! Suddenly, as your coffin is engulfed by flames, someone leaps into the flames, smashes open the coffin, and despite the most horrific burns that scar him for ever, retrieves your corpse, breathes life into your body, washes you and clothes you in his own clothes, tenderly carries you to his chauffeur-driven Bentley and takes you home to his father's presidential palace, to stay in his rooms and feast at his table, enjoying the abundant hospitality of his father for ever. That is every Christian's personal story, magnified both by the horrors of hell from which we've been rescued, and the privileges to which we've been exalted.

In the new creation, we shall find God unceasingly marvellous and delightful, our most satisfying joy. J.C. Ryle wrote:

"Let us not be afraid to **meditate** often on the subject of heaven, and to rejoice in the prospect of good things to come. I know that even a believer's heart will sometimes fail when he thinks of the last enemy which is death and the unseen world beyond. **Jordan** is a cold river to cross at best, and not a few tremble when they think of their own crossing. But let us take comfort in the remembrance of the other side. Think Christian believer, of seeing your Saviour, and beholding your King in his beauty. Faith will at last be swallowed up in sight and hope in certainty. Think of the many loved ones gone before you, and of the happy meeting between you and them. You are not going to a foreign country; you are going home. You are not going to dwell amongst strangers, but among friends. You will find them all safe, all well, all ready to greet you all prepared to join in one unbroken song of praise. Then let us take comfort and persevere. With such prospects before us, we may well cry, 'It is worthwhile being a Christian'." (*Heaven*, page 48)

Grace Alone

So now we can appreciate why Paul so excitedly emphasises that we're saved by grace alone (**v 8-10**): "It is by grace you have been saved..." (**v 8**). Our salvation is entirely God's generous and costly gift. We receive it "through faith ... the gift of God" (**v 8**). God's grace is the whole origin of our salvation—the faith created in us by his work is what enables us to receive his salvation. Like any good preacher, Paul clarifies with a negative: it is "not by works ... no one can boast" (**v 9**). We're not saved as a reward for our good deeds, our religious performance, or our church ministry. We've nothing to boast about (except the cross of Christ, Galatians 6:14)—whether in cocky self-confidence before God, arrogance towards unbelievers, or competition with other Christians. We were not saved, and will never be kept saved, by our good works of service, but by Christ's good works of service.

But the good works of Christ have saved us *for* doing good works in gratitude, for we are now "created in Christ Jesus to do good works" (Ephesians **2:10**). We've been recreated by God's Spirit through the gospel because of a reason and for a purpose: the reason was God's grace expressed in Christ's life of good works unto death for us, and the purpose is the good works prepared for us to do in gratitude to him. Understanding this distinction is enormously important. To know I am saved completely by God's grace in Christ liberates me from the pride of imagining I can save myself, and from the terror of realising that I can't!

> To know I am saved by grace liberates me from the pride of imagining I can save myself, and the terror of realising that I can't.

And to know that I've been saved for good works prepared by God liberates me from a lazy and loveless disengagement from the needs of the world, especially for the gospel, and also from ever feeling insignificant or useless. God has prepared good and different things for every one of us to do, as members of his gathering church.

This distinction has also been hugely important in church history. The word "grace" is a bit like the word "football", which means gridiron in America, rugby league in Australia and soccer in Britain. Beware of the Roman Catholic misunderstanding of grace as God's power received through church sacraments (such as "the **mass**") to enable us to become enough like Christ to get into heaven (with a bit more suffering in **purgatory**). The contrasting biblical principles of salvation by grace reflected in Ephesians are often summarised under the helpful mnemonic, TULIP, standing for:

- ■ "Total depravity"—our nature is corrupted in every part.

- ■ "Unconditional election"—God chose us although we had nothing to qualify us.

- ■ "Limited **atonement**"—a bad name for the great truth that Christ died for his particular people.

- ■ "Irresistible grace"—meaning that God can melt our resistance to him.

- ■ "Perseverance of the **saints**"—the sensational truth that God will keep his people trusting to the end despite our periods of rebellion.

Remember that the biblical idea of grace is the undeserved kindness of God in giving us what we don't have in ourselves or deserve to receive, especially the righteousness of Christ: *God's Righteousness At Christ's Expense*. Or, as great **theologians** from the past have summarised so clearly, we are saved by grace alone, in Christ alone, through faith alone, according to Scripture alone, for the glory of God alone. Where is this stunning grace available? Not in the church, but "in Christ Jesus" (**v 6, 10**).

So let's stop boasting and start celebrating God's amazing grace. And let's stop doing ministry to save ourselves and start doing it to thank our Saviour. We delight in serving Jesus not to be saved, but because we have been saved! We've been saved from death by nature, for life by grace. Can you see now why God's grace is truly "Amazing Grace"?

Questions for reflection

1. Have you passed from death to life, or are you either ignoring eternity or trusting your own efforts to take you there? Do you need the God of grace to give you life in Christ?

2. How would you use these verses to explain the gospel to a non-Christian friend in one minute?

3. How could verse 10 transform mundane or boring tasks which you do in the course of your everyday life?

4. A NEW HUMANITY

There's a depressingly relentless cycle of political strife and military conflict between the nations and religious cultures of our world. Just recently, for example, Afghanistan, Iraq, Syria, Sudan, Nigeria, North Korea, Israel and Ukraine have all experienced eruptions of violence. And there's constant suspicion and segregation between the various communities of our cities—between black and white, rich and poor, Muslim and Hindu, right-wing and left-wing. The list goes on. And then there are the tensions between colleagues in our offices, and so much cruelty and hurt in our homes.

Could our species ever stop fighting? Could there ever be lasting peace within our communities and between our cultures?

Impossible as it sounds, the answer is: *Yes*. I've met Palestinians who once fought for the Palestinian Liberation Organisation, now working alongside Israelis distributing bread in the West Bank—because they've all become Christians. Once they were implacable enemies who hated each other. Now they're brothers in the same global family of God, working together in the cause of Christ. How is that possible?

How Lasting Peace is Possible

Paul has been explaining that through Christ we can be reconciled to God, brought from death to life by grace (2:1-10). Now he turns to explain how in Christ even the most hostile enemies can be reconciled to each other in the church of God (**v 11-22**). This passage explains how our churches can gather people from diverse ethnic and social backgrounds in a miraculous way, which is absolutely impossible except through Jesus. It reveals how the cross of Christ offers lasting peace both vertically with God and horizontally with each other, imperfectly now but perfectly in the coming kingdom of the Prince of Peace.

The structure of the second half of chapter 2 is similar to that of the first half. Paul describes how hopeless our situation was without Christ (**v 11-12**, as in v 1-3), before announcing the stunning "but now" of God's grace (**v 13**, and similarly in v 4), and then explaining how God has completely transformed our situation in Christ (**v 13-22**, as in v 4-10).

Outsiders

Paul begins: "Therefore...". He's saying: *Considering your spectacular spiritual blessings in Christ (1:3-23), into which we were brought from death to life by grace alone (2:1-10), I want you to* "remember that formerly you who are Gentiles [non-Jews] by birth and called 'uncircumcised' by those who call themselves 'the **circumcision**' [Jews] (which is done in the body by human hands)—remember that at that time..." (**v 11-12**). We must pause to understand Paul's description of Gentiles here.

Paul is referring to the ceremony of circumcision of Jewish baby boys, which was symbolic of being cut free from sin with Israel. It was the sign that recalled the great gospel promise made by God to **Abraham**, that his descendants would become a blessed kingdom (Genesis 12:1-3; 17:1-14). Unfortunately, this sign had become for Jews a source of improper pride in themselves and scorn towards Gentiles, despite the repeated challenges of the prophets to remember that God intended the external ceremony to be accompanied by an interior circumcision of the heart in being cut off from sin and for Gentiles to be welcomed into God's kingdom. Paul, himself once the most brilliant Jewish scholar of his generation, diminishes ritual circumcision here by calling it that "which is done in the body by human hands", a merely human ceremony (Ephesians **2:11**). It was not being accompanied by the interior and spiritual cutting free from sin that God desired (which is now done in the hearts of Christians by the Spirit of God).

Nevertheless, at least the Jews knew about the LORD from his law. The Gentiles didn't. Paul reminds his Gentile readers of their desperate condition without Jesus—in being hopelessly distant from God's people—not to humiliate them, but to remind them of how generously they've been blessed in Christ. He describes unbelievers without Christ as living in spiritual alienation from God's people. We Westerners tend to imagine ourselves entitled to all privileges. But Paul shows that Gentiles have no right to any blessings from God. He says: "You were…"

- *"Separate from Christ"* (**v 12**): Gentiles had no share in the benefits of the exciting promises to the Jewish people of a great Christ (or "Messiah", meaning "anointed" or "chosen" one), the divine peace-making King who, after centuries of Israel waiting for him, had now arrived in Jesus. Although it was promised that Christ would bless the nations, the promise was not made to Gentiles but to Israel. We should remember this! Many British people speak of Jesus as if he were merely a part of our historical heritage, now to be ignored and consigned to the British Museum. Paul reminds us that Gentiles had no right to benefit from the peace-making Christ. Moreover, we Gentiles were…

- *"Excluded from citizenship in Israel"* (**v 12**): Gentiles had no right to citizenship among the people of God. We had no rights to the privileges of Israel in knowing God or his **covenant** promises, his ethical laws, his powerful protection or his faithful provision. Our Western pride is offended by such exclusion, but this is God's world, so we can complain as vigorously as we like to the Equalities Commission, United Nations or Supreme Court, but they cannot secure citizenship in the people of God for us.

- *"Foreigners to the covenants of the promise"* (**v 12**): God made one marvellous gospel promise to Abraham, that he and his descendants would enjoy the blessings of God's kingdom (Genesis 12:1-3), which was amplified periodically by covenant arrangements revealed progressively throughout the history of God's people. After the flood God covenanted with Noah, a man he counted "righteous" (Genesis 6:9), that he would never again destroy the world by water (9:12-16); with Abraham, who believed God's promise, he covenanted to establish the kingdom of God, through which all nations would be blessed (12:1-3); with Moses, who preferred loyalty to God's people to the comforts of this world, God covenanted at Mount Sinai to bless those who keep his law (Exodus 19:5-6); with Phinehas, who was zealous for God's glory among the Israelites travelling to the promised land, he covenanted always to provide a priest to **mediate** for sinners (Numbers 25:10-13); with David, the humble king after God's own heart, he covenanted that David's son would also be God's son ruling over God's eternal kingdom (2 Samuel 7:11-16); and to Jeremiah, the messenger who remained faithful through persecution, he promised a new covenant, announced at Jesus' last meal, established by his death and remembered in the "Lord's Supper" (Jeremiah 31:31-34). In this new covenant, God promised that his people would love obeying him, be enabled to serve him, and personally know him, because their sins would be forgiven. Jesus became entitled to all these covenant privileges—because he was perfectly righteous, believing, loyal, zealous, humble and faithful. Christ now shares these glorious privileges with all who make him their King. But without Jesus, we who are Gentiles were strangers and "foreigners" to these covenantal blessings, deserving only judgment from God. And so, writes Paul, we were...

■ *"Without hope and without God in the world"* (Ephesians **2:12**): Long ago, the Greek writer Theocritus wrote: "Hopes are for the living; the dead are without hope". Many centuries later, despair in the face of death remains as overwhelming as ever. Dylan Thomas famously protested at the passing of his father:

"Do not go gentle into that good night.

Rage, rage against the dying of the light."

And W.H. Auden expressed the hopelessness of unbelieving grief with those moving words:

"Stop all the clocks, cut off the telephone ...

Bring out the coffin, let the mourners come."

For all our impressive technology and desperate dieting, we cannot escape "**the grim reaper**"—every one of us will die. Western society has no sensible basis for confidence in life beyond the grave. So while secular atheists like Richard Dawkins, the late Christopher Hitchens and Stephen Fry defiantly try to persuade us to accept death without God, most unbelievers can only try to "eat, drink and be merry for tomorrow we die!"—to party like mad, live for now, and try not to think about death. How different this is for Christians. We have the most precious thing in all this world: hope for the next! At a thanksgiving funeral service at our church recently, for the disabled son of a Christian couple, the grieving father asked me to respond to the many kind condolences from unbelieving friends. "They tell me: 'At least you have some memories!'" he said. "But I have much more than memories. I have hope: because of Jesus, I will see my boy again, fit and well in the new creation."

> We have the most precious thing in all this world: hope for the next!

It is very striking that at christenings and weddings, unbelievers have lots of jovial things to say and everyone is happily filming with cameras and mobile phones. But at funerals, all that noisy confidence gives way to desperate tears and gloomy silence, and all that's left are memories—unless it's the funeral of a Christian. Believers know that death is not the end, and we know that those who have died trusting Christ are happy with God. To be without hope and without God in the world is especially miserable when we ourselves come to the front of the queue for the crematorium.

Without Christ, we Gentiles were without hope for eternity and without God in this world. "But now" (**v 13**) everything has changed...

Reconciled

Paul has already described the mighty reconciliation of sinners to God (v 1-10). Now he celebrates the mighty reconciliation of Christians from all nations to each other: "But now in Christ Jesus you who once were far away have been brought near by the blood of Christ" (**v 13**).

Paul is building to the climax of the first half of his letter. "But now"—despite the hopelessness of our condition—"in Christ Jesus"—united by faith to him—we who once were far from God and his people have been "brought near" to God and his people through Jesus' self-sacrifice for our sins. In Romans, the aspect of the gospel Paul emphasises is that in Christ God has given us the righteousness we lack. In Ephesians the aspect of the gospel he highlights is that in Christ we who were far away have been brought near to God and to each other. Paul now explains who brought us near, how he did it and why he did such a loving thing.

First, "he himself is our peace" (**v 14**). This celebration is all about Jesus; three times in this section Paul intensifies his focus by saying "[Christ] himself"—who not only gives peace but is himself the person in whom we find peace with God and each other. Amazingly, Christ has united the two most deeply separated categories of humanity in world history, Jews and Gentiles, into one entirely new people, central to his grand plan to unite all things under Christ. Christ has founded a whole new humanity called "Christians". Without him, the hostility between Jew and Gentile is as obvious now as ever in Israel. It has been dramatically expressed recently in the construction of the hugely controversial defensive wall built by Israel around Jerusalem. In spiritual terms, the "barrier" or "dividing wall of hostility" (**v 14**) between Jew and Gentile is the law of Moses, which the Jewish religious leaders had turned from being a sign to the world of the goodness of God into a barrier excluding the world from God's good government.

Yet the same Old Testament that contained God's law had also promised a "Prince of Peace" greater even than Solomon, the king who established earthly peace with Israel's neighbours. Paul proclaims the "gospel of peace" (6:15)—that Christ "is our peace" (**2:14**), the origin of real peace in our lives today. Deep and lasting reconciliation within marriages, families and communities was never found under Roman military domination despite its famous boast of providing *Pax Romana* (Roman Peace), nor in any other social solution. Deep inner peace is only to be found where there is spiritual dependence upon Christ crucified. For the peace of Christ is not just a negotiated absence of conflict. It's the positive harmony empowered within us by the Spirit of the divine Prince of Peace.

The historic dividing wall of God's covenant law excluding Gentiles from the people of God and his heavenly kingdom has finally been dismantled by Christ. He fulfilled all the terms of the law in his life, and then in his death exhausted its condemnation of Jew and Gentile. The death of Christ has ended the exclusion of Gentiles, because now we can all be saved on the same basis—Christ's perfect fulfilment of all the law's requirements, including the punishment of our sins.

Reinventing the Human Race

Christ's intention was nothing short of completely reinventing our human race: "to create in himself one new humanity out of the two, thus making peace" (**v 15**). When we become a Christian, we're spiritually reborn, as a new creation and part of a new human race! The church is not just a mix of Jews and Gentiles—it consists of a whole new species of being, reconciled to each other and to God (**v 16**). Paul's original Greek word used here (*apokatallaze*) is specially intensified to mean we're "super-reconciled" to God, because he's been super-satisfied by the sacrifice of his Son. What sweet joy this brings to us!

A former soldier and prison guard who recently came to faith at our church testified publicly: "I've done such terrible things in my life, but now hearing how Christ has died for my forgiveness, I can't stop crying every day for joy". Whoever we are, whatever we've done, we can be saved, but only on the same basis as everyone else—the death of Christ. It is this common dependence which brings us together in our churches.

> Whoever we are, whatever we've done, we can be saved— but only on the same basis as everyone else.

It is only Christ who brings peace. He was the one who "came and preached peace to you who were far away and peace to those who were near" (**v 17**). The LORD had proclaimed in Isaiah 52:7: "How beautiful on the mountains are the feet of those who bring good news, who proclaim peace, who bring good tidings, who proclaim salvation"; and he had promised in Isaiah 57:19: "Peace, peace, to those far and near". Christ was this beautiful **evangelist** proclaiming peace with God to all nations. So after his death and resurrection, he repeatedly appeared to his followers, saying: "Peace be with you!" with far more significance than a customary greeting (John 20:19, 21, 26). However near or far away from God we were— whether Jew or Gentile—through Christ we can have "access" to God (there's no other route to salvation for Jews or anyone else). There is therefore no room for racial pride, but there is a glorious reconciliation in knowing Christ, "through the cross, by which he put to death [our] hostility" (Ephesians **2:16**).

Jew and Gentile alike now share access together, not into a temple building in Jerusalem, but directly to our Father in heaven: "For through him we both have access to the Father by one Spirit" (**v 18**). By the work of the Son on the cross, preached to our hearts by his Spirit, we now enjoy constant access to our loving heavenly Father in prayer.

Our recognition of needing the death of Jesus to be reconciled to God is what empowers our humble willingness to be reconciled to each other. So if we're finding it difficult to be at peace with others, perhaps because we've been hurt so deeply or so often by them, we will need time in prayer to seek strength from Jesus, who has loved us enough to reconcile us to God with his blood. For from his reconciliation of sinners to the Father comes the spiritual power for reconciliation with each other.

Questions for reflection

1. How have you seen, or experienced, gospel-centred reconciliation between people?

2. Are there aspects of your background—nationality, ethnicity, social class, education—that you use as a barrier to divide yourself from other Christians (perhaps subconsciously), because you overvalue these things as being intrinsic to your identity?

3. Is there another Christian who has hurt you deeply? How does looking at what Jesus did on the cross empower you to forgive them? How could you seek to pursue reconciliation with them?

PART TWO

When we look at the motley crew of stunningly ordinary people, many very broken, who gather in our local churches, we might wonder why the Lord of heaven and earth would bother with us. Wouldn't he prefer something more impressive that reflects his glory and power? Wouldn't he want vast crowds of A-list celebrities and successful superstars crammed into majestic cathedrals, stunning mega-churches and famous stadiums? In this passage, however, Paul reveals God's extraordinary passion for ordinary churches. We discover that every congregation of sinners, forgiven and gathered together under Christ through the gospel, is actually his magnificent temple dwelling (**v 21**). The consequences are staggering.

The Temple of God

Being a spiritual temple of the living Lord has three dimensions to it, which Paul explores in turn. The believers of this Gentile church are now welcomed into the people and family of God, founded on the gospel of Christ, and constructed as a dwelling for his Spirit.

First, we are *welcomed:* "Consequently you are no longer foreigners and strangers, but fellow citizens with God's people and also members of his household" (**v 19**). As rebels, we were all once "foreigners and strangers" to God, excluded from the joys of his people and from any comfort in his family. But now, we share in Christ's spectacular privileges in his kingdom and family. We're not illegal immigrants dodging the border guards, but "fellow-citizens" of heaven, enjoying an eternal freedom to remain, passports stamped with the King's blood, entitled to all the benefits of the new-creation paradise. We're no longer primarily Canadian, Nigerian or Polish but Christians! And the homeland we all long for is no longer the green fields of England, the white beaches of Australia, the red earth of South Africa or the misty mountains of Korea. We're primarily citizens of heaven, currently travelling away from our heavenly home on the earth for gospel business.

This gathering of diverse peoples in the heavenly church according to God's plan (1:10) has massive implications for our churches on earth. We won't be content only to reach people like ourselves. We will want to make disciples from a diversity of cultural and social backgrounds because this exalts the work of Christ, as well as enriching our church life. This must not be misrepresented as a charter for the inclusion of unrepentantly sinful cultures or for guilt about the social character of our own church. However, Jesus did not say: "Make disciples of your own

> Jesus did *not* say: *Make disciples of your own kind.*

kind" but: "Make disciples of all nations" (Matthew 28:19). When planting new churches it's wise to be intentional about starting with a culture appropriate to the community being evangelised and being willing to become "all things to all people so that by all possible means I might save some" (1 Corinthians 9:22). However, although every church will inevitably develop its own distinctive culture, churches should embrace God's commitment to diversity because the gospel is for all.

Churches can't be equally effective at reaching into all the segregated communities of our society at the same time, because all kinds of cultural choices must be made in running meetings and programmes. And churches shouldn't feel embarrassed about the particular social community or communities in which God has placed them. But gospel churches will want to encourage their members in a cross-cultural missionary outlook locally as well as internationally, and will want to support multicultural church multiplication wherever it can—because the cultural diversity of earthly churches is an exaltation of Christ.

Indeed, the growing diversity of churches is necessary to reach people of all nations in our neighbourhoods; it is attractive to most unbelievers, and despite the inevitable cultural challenges, hugely enjoyable for members of the church. The heavenly church is certainly not a neat box of perfectly identical, shiny gold-wrapped chocolates all in a row, but a mixed-up, multicoloured collection of "liquorice all-sorts". Earthly churches will aspire to the same cultural hospitality; for once we were all "foreigners and strangers" (Ephesians **2:19**), but now we're all welcomed into the same multicultural family.

Christians are now "members of [God's] household" (**v 19**), adopted as children and heirs of the Father, brothers and sisters of Jesus, to be loved, protected, disciplined and lavishly cared for by God for ever. Indeed, we no longer derive our family identity, security and guidance primarily from our earthly families. A grieving disciple called by Jesus protested: "'Lord, first let me go and bury my father.' But Jesus told him, 'Follow me, and let the dead bury their own dead'" (Matthew 8:21-22)! Belonging to God's heavenly family also has massive implications for our churches, which are perhaps more challenging the larger our church becomes. For however professionally organised we must become, we must still behave like family, with appreciative respect, pure affection and sacrificial kindness towards each other. We need to be there for each other, offering the warm support that many of us cannot expect from our earthly families. Not long ago, a girl from a Muslim family came to our church and began to follow Jesus. Having become estranged from and threatened by her Muslim family because she'd become a Christian, she was given a home and then given away on her wedding day by one of our church elders. The church had become her family.

The Unchanging Foundation

Second, we are *founded* on the gospel of Christ. To be a church, we must be "built on the foundation of the apostles and prophets, with Christ Jesus himself as the chief cornerstone" (Ephesians **2:20**). The heavenly church, expressed in all its local congregations on earth, is founded upon the teaching of the first-century apostles of Christ, who announced the gospel of God, and the first-century prophets, who explained the word of God (see 4:11).

There is some debate over who and what "prophets" and "prophecy" mean. My own view is that the privilege of prophesying by the power of the Holy Spirit was given to all believers at Pentecost (Acts 2—as promised by Joel), and involves proclaiming Jesus from the Bible (as Peter did at Pentecost). The gift of excelling in such prophecy (described in 1 Corinthians 14) consists in God-given revelations of insight into the Scriptures such as will be especially evident in some believers in our Bible studies and church meetings. Ever since the teachings of Christ and his apostles and prophets recorded in Scriptures, prophecy seems to be God-given insight into the completed revelation of God in Scripture, rather than additional pictures and messages, for "the Spirit of prophecy ... bears testimony to Jesus" (Revelation 19:10).

After all, as Paul points out, churches can only be built in accordance with the gospel of Christ himself as the chief cornerstone (Ephesians **2:20**). Christ gives the decisive shape to the whole foundation and the building constructed upon it. This fulfils the LORD's promise: "See, I lay a stone in **Zion**, a tested stone, a precious cornerstone for a sure foundation" (Isaiah 28:16). This tested stone in Zion is not just Christ, but Christ "tested" and proved to be precious in Jerusalem on the cross. The heavenly church—and every genuine, earthly, local church—is founded on this gospel of this tested Christ.

Jesus had already said this in Matthew 16, when Peter blurted out his God-given recognition of Jesus: "You are the Messiah, the Son of the living God", to which Jesus responded: "I tell you that you are Peter, and on this rock I will build my church" (v 16, 18). The rock Jesus refers to represents Peter's gospel—his confession that Jesus is the Christ, the son of God (and not the rock of Mount Sinai, where the church of Israel had once gathered to receive the law). Jesus had earlier explained in his Sermon on the Mount that the person who lives by his teaching is like a wise man building his house on stable rock, rather than shifting sand (Matthew 7:24-27). Christ is the ultimate wise man, building his own house on the rock of the gospel.

Your Church's One Foundation

What does this mean for your church today? First, the foundation is finished: it has already been laid and Christ's church is being built upon it. There'll be no new foundation, and every new church planted today must be founded on this gospel rock of Scripture, or it's not part of the heavenly church. We will keep discovering more in the Bible, but we're not hearing new guidance from God in our hearts or in our imagination upon which to build Christ's church. We are also not developing **trajectories** from Scripture to today in order to create more culturally acceptable foundations for the church. The foundational teaching of Christ and his apostles and prophets is completed and available in Scripture, and Christ has been building his church on it for 2,000 years. God is not constantly relocating his church upon alternative foundations, but building up his church upon the one original and completed foundation in the Bible. It's God's building, and he has completed its foundations.

Second, this foundation is sufficient: Christ is building his church upon his gospel in Scripture, and it doesn't need improving or adapting. We're not at liberty to dig up the foundations of God's building and start again in every age, directed by the popular gurus of our day. It's not too big and in need of reduction—so we're not free to remove unpopular truths about the uniqueness of Christ, the eternity of hell, the need for sexual restraint or the heterosexual nature of marriage. Neither is it too small and in need of additional doctrine, whether that is based on ancient traditions about Mary or the contemporary "revelations" of a healing conference. The foundational gospel of the Bible is all the revelation that the church needs today.

Great damage can come from churches trying to supplement these foundations. In 1934 in Germany, the "Confessing Churches", led by Barth, Bonhoeffer and Niemoller, produced a brilliant statement called the "Barmen Declaration", stoutly resisting the idea that God was leading his church into new truth through the National Socialism of Adolf Hitler. Barmen declared:

> "We reject the false doctrine, as though the church could and would have to acknowledge as a source of its proclamation, apart from and besides this one word of God, still other events and powers, figures and truths, as God's revelation."

These dangers can be very personal. I once met a girl who was devastated that the "ministry to the rich and famous" that someone had absurdly promised her in a "word" from a prophetic ministries convention had never materialised! Of course, it's far easier to spot the foundations being altered in other churches. Far more challenging is to check our own foundation: are we removing anything in Scripture by ignoring it? Are we adding anything to it by insisting on it? The teaching of the Bible is the finished foundation of Christ's church.

Third, this foundation is saving: churches must continue to proclaim this foundational gospel teaching as the rock upon which men and women, young and old, can build their lives with confidence that they're safe from the storm to come. All other "gospels" and all other teaching are sinking sand that cannot save anyone.

A Dwelling for the Spirit

Lastly, the church of Christ is *constructed*. "In him the whole building is joined together and rises to become a holy temple in the Lord. And in him you too are being built together to become a dwelling in which God lives by his Spirit" (Ephesians **2:21-22**)

The heavenly church is the home of God—his dwelling place, which was symbolised in Israel by the temple in Jerusalem. The last temple in Jerusalem, built by Herod the Great, was a wonder of the ancient world. It was constructed of enormous white marble blocks, inlaid with gold that sparkled in the sunshine for miles around. God had promised a building that would be his home, where he'd dwell among his people—his palace, from where he'd govern them, and his temple, where he'd receive sacrifices for their forgiveness.

Ultimately, he fulfilled his promises not in a building, but in a person. The temple took human form when God took flesh in Jesus. He "tabernacled" among us (see John 1:14)—and Jesus declared that the temple of his body would be destroyed and raised again in three days (John 2:19-22). And this human temple would be the site of the ultimate sacrifice, when Christ shed his blood and presented it to his Father as the sin-bearing offering for his people at Calvary.

Now united by faith with Jesus, every Christian is a temple, and every church is a temple of the Holy Spirit—a magnificent wonder of the modern world. We may meet in a crumby school hall, a medieval stone building, or a leaky corrugated-iron hut. But every gathered assembly of God's people is God's temple, his dwelling-place among us; his palace, where he governs us; and his temple, where we celebrate the finished sacrifice of Jesus.

> Every church is a temple of the Spirit—a magnificent wonder of the world.

And since God is holy, separate from sin in the beauty of his goodness, God is gradually refurbishing his home in our hearts and churches, to suit his holy character, by his Spirit through his word. Christ wants his churches to be welcoming to strangers, faithful to their gospel foundation and increasingly holy. He wants churches that provide a little foretaste of the glory of heaven!

This is only possible "in him", who is Jesus Christ our Lord (Ephesians **2:21, 22**, and similarly in **v 15, 16, 18**). It's as we get to know him in Scripture, remain in him by faith, and obey him in life that he builds his churches to become holy like him, for he is the eternal temple (Revelation 21:22). Every local church—however unimpressive the people, however painful the music, however tatty the building— is a spiritually beautiful expression of the glorious church of God in heaven. In fact, each is intended to prepare God's people for that vast and spectacular multicultural festival that is the heavenly church. Each one demonstrates in the heavenly realms the awesome power and victory of God over evil powers to accomplish his eternal plan to bring everything together under Christ through his reconciling death.

So, next time you attend your church, however ordinary the people may seem, however unimpressive the building may look, remember the three glorious spiritual dimensions of your church: you're welcomed into the precious family of God, so love those people deeply; you're being built upon the foundation of the Scriptures, so listen to the teaching carefully; and you're being constructed as a dwelling of the Spirit of God, so be holy in the way you behave. Your local church is a gathering of a new humanity, the temple of the living God, the only "local building" that will last for ever, and a wonder in the heavenly realms. Enjoy it!

Questions for reflection

1. How has this passage reshaped your view of your own church?

2. Are you, or is your church, in danger of adding to Scripture or removing something from Scripture as the sufficient foundation for your life together? (If not, what do you think would be the most likely way for such a thing to happen without people noticing?)

3. Love your church family deeply… listen to the teaching carefully… be holy in the way you behave… Are you struggling in one of those areas particularly? How will the truths about your church highlighted in this passage motivate you towards greater love, listening and holiness?

5. THE MYSTERY REVEALED

Most of us enjoy the suspense of a mystery thriller—perhaps an old Agatha Christie novel like *Murder on the Nile* or a classic Hitchcock film such as *Rear Window*, or perhaps a more contemporary TV crime-investigation series like *CSI Miami* or a more hard-edged "Nordic noir" serial-killer series. And surely everyone's intrigued by those enduring, unsolved mysteries of the famous "Loch Ness Monster" in Scotland, or "Bigfoot" in California. Other mysteries are more personal—like how to fill in your tax form or knowing what your wife really wanted for Christmas!

The only thing *more* compelling than a mystery is when the mystery finally gets solved. The apostle Paul explains in this extraordinary passage that there had been a perplexing mystery troubling Israel for centuries, concerning God's salvation plan—a mystery now solved in the most astonishing fashion by the coming of Christ. Indeed, the solution to this mystery is displayed in the spiritual realms for all to admire God's wisdom. This passage is critical for understanding Paul's letter to the Ephesians, and especially for understanding the ministry of the apostle Paul.

Revealed, not Evolving

There is a view gaining traction in some circles that the Bible offers evolving "trajectories", that continue his revelation beyond the completion of the Bible to today. This tends to involve us conveniently concluding that God is now saying something culturally acceptable that contradicts the inconvenient things he once said in the Bible. For example, it is suggested that if God's people in the Old Testament included Jews but not Gentiles, and then the New Testament said that God's people can include Gentiles but not those living unrepentantly in greed or sexual immorality, then we're now at liberty to continue that trajectory ourselves and conclude that God's people can now include those living unrepentantly after all. In this way of thinking, the parts of the Bible that we find difficult to accept are declared to be mysteries which we can solve today.

But our text presents a wholly different approach which reflects the teaching of Jesus. Paul says that God's mystery has now been "revealed" (**3:5**). Of course, we will keep discovering things we hadn't realised about Christ in the Bible, but God's eternal purposes have all been "accomplished in Christ Jesus" (**v 11**). Jesus and his apostles consistently teach that all the Old Testament mysteries were solved and fulfilled in the words and works of Christ in the New Testament; the trajectory was from the promises of the Old Testament to their fulfilment in the gospel of the New Testament! The mysteries are all solved in him—or as Paul writes here: "... the mystery of Christ, which was not made known to people in other generations as it has now been revealed by the Spirit to God's holy apostles and prophets" (**v 4-5**).

> Our gospel is not guesswork and theory, but fact and truth.

Our privilege today is not to invent evolving mysteries and trajectories that we can solve the way we want, as if we are the next act in the unfolding drama of God's revelation (as some scholars mischievously claim). Our privilege is to proclaim the glorious fulfilment of all the trajectories, and the solving of all salvation mysteries, in Christ. Indeed, the Bible is a classic mystery-suspense thriller—all is revealed in the end! And the person responsible is not a suspicious butler full of vengeance, but a crucified Saviour full of love. Our gospel is not guesswork and theory, but fact and truth! That is what Paul celebrates in this sensational passage.

Paul's Prison Ministry

In **verse 1**, Paul begins: "For this reason", because, having explained how Christ's death and resurrection have reconciled people to God and to each other (chapter 2), he is about to explain what he therefore prays for the Ephesians: "For this reason I, Paul, the prisoner of Christ Jesus for the sake of you Gentiles..." But then he realises that he must break off to explain what he means in saying he is a prisoner for their sake. He needs to explain his own role in God's plan to save Gentiles (and he will resume explaining his prayers later—in 3:14, where he returns to the words of **verse 1**: "For this reason I kneel...").

So Paul breaks off to explain his ministry, strengthen his relationship with them by describing his commitment to them, and reassure them that his imprisonment shouldn't cast doubt upon his message or his ministry because he was authorised by God to announce the astonishing "mystery made known to me by revelation" (**v 3**), by which Gentiles can be saved. Indeed, this mystery is what reveals the triumphant wisdom of God's eternal plan for his church in the spiritual realms (**v 10**). He completes his **digression** in **verse 13** when he feels able to conclude: "I ask you, therefore, not to be discouraged because of my sufferings for you".

It is very striking how this persecuted man in prison, far from feeling sorry for himself, three times bubbles up with gratitude for God's grace given to him (**v 2, 7, 8**)—because he knows he is part of God's extraordinary plan for saving people from all nations. And so Paul excitedly explains to whom God revealed his glorious mystery (**v 2-5**); what the mystery really is (**v 6**); and why this mystery must now be proclaimed to all nations, whatever the cost (**v 7-9**).

Revealing the Mystery

Paul assumes that his readers from various churches in the region of Ephesus must all have heard the amazing reports of how the risen Jesus had dramatically confronted and transformed him on his way to Damascus to persecute Christians. Paul says Jesus revealed to him "the administration of God's grace ... for you" (**v 2**). "Administration" refers to the way God's grace is made available to Gentiles through Christ's death on a cross, proclaimed by a persecuted preacher! It wasn't Paul's message about the grace of God being given to Gentiles that got Paul in trouble, nor even that it was available to Jews and Gentiles through a Messiah (or "Christ"). It was "the administration" (meaning "economy" or "strategy" or "stewardship") of God's saving grace—offered through a man executed by the Jewish leaders on a criminal's cross, without any obligation to become Jewish, and announced by God through missionary apostles—that really was offensive to Jewish leaders (for reasons we shall soon examine).

So in **verse 3**, Paul clarifies how he learned "the mystery made known to me by revelation, as I have already written briefly". This mystery of how Gentiles and Jews can be saved in Christ was revealed as directly to Paul by Christ as to the other apostles, who accompanied Jesus on his missions. Paul is keen to establish that his gospel came by divine "revelation" and not human "invention", as he had already briefly written—he's probably thinking of what he's already written in this letter (1:1, 9-10) rather than in other letters. This brings Paul to his main point: "In reading this, then, you will be able to understand my insight into the mystery of Christ, which was not made known ... as it has now been revealed by the Spirit to God's holy apostles and prophets" (**3:4-5**). Paul wants his readers to recognise that he'd been given special insight into "the mystery of Christ" by God.

But Paul also says elsewhere that the gospel was "promised beforehand through the prophets in the Holy Scriptures" (Romans 1:2); so why does he say here that the mystery of the gospel wasn't previously known? Doesn't this sound like so many false religious prophets, such as Muhammad of Islam or Joseph Smith of Mormonism, or indeed more recently, the now-discredited Kansas City Prophets, who all claimed special insights from God? Actually, Paul wasn't proclaiming a new gospel. The gospel of blessing for all nations in God's kingdom had been announced to Abraham, and promised by the prophets; for example: "How beautiful on the mountains are the feet of those who bring good news, who proclaim peace, who say to Zion, 'Your God reigns!' ... and all the ends of the earth will see the salvation of our God" (Isaiah 52:7, 10).

What was completely unknown and inaccessible to human understanding was not God's plan to save all nations, but how God could accomplish such a plan. That was a complete mystery!

This great mystery had now finally been revealed to the apostles, including Paul. Gentiles could be saved because in his death, Christ completed his righteous life for Jew and Gentile alike, and suffered God's wrath on the cross for the sins of his Jewish and Gentile people alike. Paul refers twice to the "administration" (better translated "strategy") of this mystery (Ephesians **3:2, 9**)—that is, how it works. God's gospel promise to bless all nations had been known since Abraham. But the strategy of how God could ever achieve this ancient plan was a complete mystery. Paul's gospel was therefore not a new gospel, but the ancient gospel revealed—that ancient gospel had at last been accomplished and clarified!

This means that the apostles were more than preachers—they weren't just being helpful to God in advertising his gospel. They had a distinctive and unique ministry that

> Paul's gospel was not a new gospel, but the ancient gospel revealed and clarified.

was always foundational to God's great salvation plan. They were given God's authority to explain how God's gospel promise was accomplished through the death and resurrection of Christ. Although the word "apostle" simply means messenger, and is very occasionally used in this general sense of an ordinary Christian teacher (Romans 16:7), it was a term generally carefully reserved for the original witnesses of the risen Christ, who were commissioned by Jesus to proclaim and clarify his gospel and write the New Testament as the foundation upon which he is building his church (Ephesians 2:20; **3:5**; 4:11). It therefore cannot be wise to call church leaders today "apostles", or to speak of them having apostolic gifts or roles. Indeed, there is a growing tendency to describe leaders as having a specially prophetic, priestly or kingly gifting (beyond the sense in which all Christians are prophets, priests and kings in Christ) which is profoundly unhelpful (and potentially offensive to God, as we learn from the story of Korah's rebels, who wanted special roles as prophets and priests among the people of Israel, and were judged because God was reserving these special roles for his Son—Numbers 16). Paul is here describing his foundational role as an original apostle, to whom the mystery of the gospel of Christ crucified was revealed by the risen Jesus; and who was given a particular responsibility as part of God's "administration" or strategy, to preach this gospel to Gentiles.

But what is the substance of this thrilling gospel mystery, revealed to the apostles?

Gentiles Included

Paul now clarifies more exactly what the mystery is: "... that through the gospel the Gentiles are heirs together with Israel, members together of one body, and sharers together in the promise in Christ Jesus" (Ephesians **3:6**).

The confusion now clarified by Paul is that Gentiles can be saved, along with Jews, without keeping the law of Israel—through faith in the crucified Christ who kept it all for us! We could easily miss how shocking this was. It was never a surprise that Gentiles could join the people of God—that had always been possible through submission to the law of Moses. Gentiles could be circumcised and join the religious disciplines of Israel. But Paul was now preaching that salvation was available without observing the law of Israel! He was proclaiming that the law wasn't intended to save people but to expose their need of a Saviour to keep the law perfectly for all who rely on him (Galatians 3:22), for neither Jew nor Gentile could ever fully keep it.

God's mystery now revealed is that "through the gospel" and not the law, Gentiles can be included among God's saved people

(Ephesians **3:6**). So anyone who repents from their sin to trust in the gospel that Jesus (the crucified **Galilean**) is the Christ (the long-promised Saviour King, who died for our sins) and their Lord (the God-man risen from the grave to rule and to judge us all) will be saved. This meant that Gentiles didn't have to become Jewish. The offence in this message—which resulted in Paul being hated by Jews who accused him of treason in order to have him imprisoned by the Romans—was not that he preached salvation to the Gentiles. The offence was preaching salvation for Gentiles simply through faith in the gospel rather than by keeping the law of Israel (though we are saved for lives of keeping "Christ's law", 1 Corinthians 9:21). This gospel also meant that Jews who were observing the law weren't saved unless they put their faith in the Christ whom their leaders had crucified. No wonder they were furious with him!

Paul explains that this salvation through faith in the gospel brings three marvellous privileges (for which Paul actually invents new words):

First, they are "heirs together" (Ephesians **3:6**)—the original text doesn't mention "with Israel" but translators often include it because Paul does teach that in Romans 11. But here in Ephesians, he is teaching that our privilege is not just to join old Israel, but to join with Jews in one completely new people in Christ, called Christians, who all now inherit the kingdom of heaven. At the end of the Bible, we are given a tantalising description of God's "Extreme Makeover" of the whole cosmos, his renewed creation prepared for our resurrection life, the garden-city paradise which will be our inheritance:

"Then the angel showed me the river of the water of life, as clear as crystal ... On each side of the river stood the tree of life, bearing twelve crops of fruit, yielding its fruit every month. And the leaves of the tree are for the healing of the nations. No longer will there be any curse. The throne of God and of the Lamb will be in the city, and his servants will serve him. They will see his face, and his name will be on their foreheads ... And they will reign for ever and ever." (Revelation 22:1-5)

Notice three spectacular features of our paradise inheritance: The river of the water of life depicts an inexhaustible torrent of life-giving spiritual abundance, forever washing us clean and filling us with thirst-quenching satisfaction from the Holy Spirit (see Ezekiel 47; John 7:38). The tree of life (literally the "wood" of life) symbolises the everlasting deliverance of the cross, and the leaves of this tree "are for the healing of the nations" (Revelation 22:2), permanently healing us from the damage of sin in our souls and the decay of death in our bodies. As the tree of life in the Garden of Eden was the source of life that looked forward to the cross on which Jesus was punished for our sins, the tree of life in the new creation looks back to the cross as the source of eternal life. His death will forever provide God's deliverance from his curse of judgment through Christ's death on the wood of a Roman cross (Ezekiel 47; Acts 5:30; 10:39; 13:29; 1 Peter 2:24).

And his servants (including us) will serve him, see him and rule with him. What a joy to finally serve him well. Just imagine seeing the face of your Saviour! And how marvellous to hear his words of approval: "Well done, good and faithful servant! ... Come and share your master's happiness!" (Matthew 25:21). The exact tone of his words and the smile on his face will live with us for ever and make every cost of following him worthwhile. Our inheritance is to be there with our Saviour in heaven, enjoying the abundance of his Spirit, the deliverance of his cross, and the privileges of his presence.

I wonder if you can grasp how epic that will be? On 4th August 2012 at the Olympic Games in London, I was fortunate to be in the Olympic stadium with three of my children when Jessica Ennis, Greg Rutherford and Mo Farah each won gold medals for Great Britain within the space of 46 glorious minutes. The noise was amazing, and the experience more fabulous than anything I have ever experienced in sport. But I whispered to my daughter at the end: "If this is what it's like praising some athletes who can throw a spear, jump a long way and run fast, how good will it be when the King of heaven comes on stage?" It will be unbelievably fabulous to be there! We will inherit all this because this is Christ's inheritance, and we will share it with him.

Questions for reflection

1. How would you explain to someone the relationship between the Old Testament and the New Testament?

2. The gospel "was not made known to people in other generations as it has now been revealed by the Spirit to God's holy apostles and prophets" (v 5). Have you ever realised that you are in a *more* privileged position than the Israelites who heard God at Mt Sinai, or even the Old Testament prophets?

3. How does being reminded of the wonderful inheritance that lies ahead of you change the way you look at both your recent successes and your current problems in this life?

PART TWO

One Body

Paul began this great epistle praising God for the sensational personal blessings of faith in Christ. Since then, he has been explaining the glorious blessings of being united in Christ with believers of every background in the people of God. He's just finished explaining that the first great privilege is to be heirs together in the kingdom of heaven. Now he explores the second glorious blessing of being "members together of one body"—in the church (Ephesians **3:6**).

Whether we are Jewish or Gentile, and whatever our racial or socio-economic background, when we became Christians we were spiritually united in Christ. We therefore all received the same Spirit of Christ to unite us together **experientially** in the life of our local church. For, since the God who created and redeemed us is **plural**, church is meant to be a team game. A church is never about one person or one kind of people.

Paul uses the image of a body because a body consisting of one foot, or even dozens of feet stitched together, could not function well! Likewise, churches need different people working together. There should be no superiority or inferiority in the limbs of a body or a church, because each one is needed. No one is in a church accidentally and no one is unnecessary—because we're put together by God's design. Churches mustn't become like gym fanatics, desperately trying to re-sculpt their bodies, or like the late Michael Jackson, who was a musical genius but kept trying to alter his appearance with plastic surgery. We should treasure the church we are part of because God designs our particular diversity in the different seasons of our church life. As our body would be useless if all our organs were kidneys or all our limbs were thumbs, so our personal diversity in church means we can do more together in our diversity than we ever could if we were all the same.

The third glorious blessing of being together in Christ that Paul explores is that, through faith in the gospel, we become "sharers together in the promise in Christ Jesus". This refers to the empowering of God's Holy Spirit, whose presence was promised in the Old Testament as the chief blessing of being the people of God (Ezekiel 36:26-27; see Ephesians 1:13-14). In the Old Testament, the Holy Spirit enabled prophets to speak, kings to rule, judges to rescue and artists to create for God. And the prophets promised a Christ filled with this same Holy Spirit: "The Spirit of the LORD will rest on him— the Spirit of wisdom and of understanding" (Isaiah 11:2). By faith in him, we share in the same Holy Spirit, who enables our ministries for Christ:

- He teaches us the truth about Christ: at his farewell meal, Jesus promised "the Spirit of truth", who "will teach you all things and will remind you of everything I have said to you" (John 14:17-26). The Spirit enabled the disciples to write the New Testament, and enables us to understand what they wrote.

- He enables us all to prophesy about Christ: in Acts 2, as promised by the prophet Joel and by Jesus, God poured out his Holy Spirit upon all his disciples to renew them. This was obvious in Jerusalem when previously terrified disciples began boldly proclaiming "the wonders of God" (v 11) done by Jesus, proclaiming him as Saviour and Lord from the Scriptures. Since then, the Spirit empowers all believers to prophesy the wonders of God in Christ by teaching the gospel from those Scriptures.

- He gives us new life in Christ: in his classic celebration of the ministry of the Spirit in Romans 8, Paul explains that the Holy Spirit brings us new government ("the mind governed by the Spirit" through his word, v 6); new life ("the Spirit gives life", v 10); new battles ("if by the Spirit you put to death the misdeeds of the body, you will live", v 13); and new confidence ("the Spirit you received brought about your adoption to sonship. And by him we cry, 'Abba, Father'", v 15); as God's Spirit convinces us of the gospel—that by faith in the Son, we are children of God.

■ He grows the fruit of Christ in us: in Galatians 5:22-23 we learn that "living by the Spirit" isn't walking around hearing messages or tingling with miraculous powers, but serving one another in love. Perfection is impossible until heaven because our sinful nature remains. But the Spirit creates internal conflict with our selfishness and organically grows in us "the fruit of the Spirit"—those beautiful Christ-like virtues of love, joy, peace, forbearance, kindness, goodness, faithfulness, gentleness and self-control.

■ He gives us gifts for serving the body of Christ: in 1 Corinthians 12 – 14, Paul celebrates Christ's "grace-gifts" (*charismata*), given to all his people for serving the church by building others up in their faith. There are many kinds of gifts: some remarkable, like healing; others mundane, like administration. No one is given them all; we may have many or few, and develop or lose them as God chooses. Most gifts are a competence to do very well what other Christians do averagely, like encouragement or "helping". With such gifts the Spirit equips us all for building up the faith of others with love.

What a stunning privilege it is to be "sharers together in the promise" of God's Holy Spirit, so that we can each contribute to the life of our local church (Ephesians **3:6**)! The mystery of the gospel reveals the grace of God to us all in Christ.

It's now obvious what to do with this mystery…

Proclaim the Mystery

Paul now draws out the implications of knowing the mystery revealed in the apostolic gospel—becoming a "servant [literally "slave"] of this gospel" (Ephesians **3:7**).

Paul is not supporting slavery here. Tragically, slavery was a common reality in his world, as it remains in ours—the UN estimates human trafficking involves 2.4 million people at any time, of which 80%

are sex slaves. Slavery is a disgusting exploitation of people who are each incredibly precious to God.

When we grasp the horror of slavery, we begin to feel the wonder of Paul's self-description—as a "slave" of God and his gospel! This ministry of slavery was received through the working of God's "power"—his dramatic experience of personal **conversion** from being a persecutor of Christians into an apostle of Christ. He describes himself in **verse 8** as "less than the least of all the Lord's people", not in false modesty or exaggerated guilt, but because he was profoundly conscious of the wickedness of his previous persecution of Christ's church. Many of us will likewise be aware of terrible things that we've done, perhaps against the children of God, and share Paul's sense of amazement at the grace of God towards us.

Paul's particular role was "to preach to the Gentiles the boundless riches of Christ" (**v 8**; Acts 9:15)—to proclaim the inexhaustible treasures of the marvellous spiritual blessings available to everyone in Christ (such as those described in Ephesians 1:1-14 and **3:6**).

The three richest people in the world are currently Bill Gates, Carlos Slim and Warren Buffett, each worth more than $70 billion. But such wealth cannot buy them one moment in heaven, and they cannot take their fortune with them (the Pharaohs tried to take their wealth with them in their pyramids, but grave-robbers got the lot). Without Christ, these billionaires will have nothing for eternity. This should make us seriously re-evaluate what kind of wealth we want to acquire for ourselves and our families.

My father doesn't have much money. But he and my mother introduced their children to Jesus. I would rather have this than any billionaire's fortune! Recently, at my dad's 80th-birthday celebration, he memorably addressed his eighteen grandchildren with these words:

"Since I became a Christian in 1947, I have not for one second had cause to regret following Jesus. Now you youngsters will come under huge pressure to follow the world, but I urge you to follow Jesus, because you will enjoy him for eternity."

My dad isn't materially rich, but he is spiritually wealthy with the "boundless riches of Christ" (**v 8**). We need to realise that spending our lives knowing Christ will prove far more enriching than amassing a vast property portfolio and spectacular holiday snaps. Many of our church staff are pitied by their friends and family for giving up highly paid careers in the City of London. But they are richer than ever before! Your local church is full of billionaires—spiritual ones, who are infinitely wealthy in "the boundless riches of Christ"!

However, Paul was called not only to proclaim the boundless riches of Christ, but "to make plain to everyone the administration ("strategy") of this mystery, which for ages past was kept hidden in God" (**v 9**). It is God's strategy of saving us through the death and resurrection of his only beloved Son, proclaimed by a despised preacher who had once been his implacable enemy, which makes God's mystery so utterly remarkable!

> Your local church is full of billionaires— spiritual ones.

I learned recently that when Winston Churchill was writing his famous war-time speech after the Battle of Britain, in which he declared: "Never in the field of human conflict has so much been owed by so many to so few", his original script read: "Never in human history has so much been owed by so many to so few". But as he was being driven to Parliament, practising his speech in the back of the car, a companion interrupted and asked: "What about Jesus and his disciples?" Churchill considered for a moment, and then changed the line to restrict it to "human conflict". Because never in human history has so much been owed by so many to so few as to Christ and his apostles. The billions of people from all nations being gathered into Christ's church to enjoy the unsearchable riches of God's grace will owe it all to Christ, as he is revealed in the mystery of the gospel that was faithfully proclaimed by his appointed apostles.

Why on earth would God ever plan such a remarkable thing?

Your Church: God's Wisdom on Display

God's purpose in the revealed mystery of the gospel of Christ and him crucified is simply breathtaking: "His intent was that now, through the church, the manifold wisdom of God should be made known to the rulers and authorities in the heavenly realms, according to his eternal purpose that he accomplished in Christ Jesus our Lord" (**v 10-11**).

The "manifold wisdom" of God is the complex brilliance of his salvation plan. This phrase conjures images of an intricately embroidered, magnificent tapestry, or the multi-faceted beauty of a priceless diamond. This beautiful wisdom of God in the gospel is displayed, for all the powers in the spiritual realms to see, in the rich diversity of a local church. Every local church is God's trophy cabinet.

One of the most powerful arguments for the truth of the gospel for sceptical unbelievers is that the same Lord Jesus is worshipped by all kinds of people gathered in all kinds of churches all over the world. Islam, Buddhism and atheism do not tend to thrive in all cultures. But the same gospel of Christ is celebrated by Christians of every nation and cultural background.

But the church is also being watched in the "heavenly realms" (**v 10**), or spiritual dimensions. There, the hostile powers of Satan are forced to recognise the triumph of God's eternal plan to gather people together in his church under Christ. Every local-church gathering anywhere in the world is like one of those open-top bus champions' celebrations: but instead of a football team celebrating a temporary sporting victory in a stadium, a church gathering under Christ is a celebration of God's eternal spiritual victory over Satan, sin and death at the cross.

Now "through faith in [Christ] we may approach God with freedom and confidence" (**v 12**). Wherever we've come from and whatever we've done, through the gospel we can confidently approach God in prayer and live in his presence, on the earth now and one day in heaven—no longer his terrified enemies, but as his precious, adopted children.

So Paul urges the Ephesians "not to be discouraged because of my sufferings for you, which are your glory" (**v 13**). There was absolutely no reason to be discouraged by Paul's imprisonment—it was all part of God's plan. The sufferings of Paul in prison for preaching Christ crucified were all part of God's glorious plan to use despised messengers to advertise the riches of his unsearchable grace in the heavenly realms! So also today, there's no need to be discouraged by the persecution of Christians in North Korea, Pakistan or Yemen, or by any hostility towards your faith. The news is out—the gospel has gone viral! Christ is building his vast heavenly church out of his growing collection of churches from every nation on earth, each celebrating his sparkling wisdom and amazing grace in the spiritual realms—even amid persecution!

The greatest mystery in history has been solved in Christ—and it is on display in his trophy cabinet: your church!

Questions for reflection

1. "No one is in a church accidentally and no one is unnecessary." Do you view yourself too highly or too lowly when it comes to your church? And who in your church needs encouragement to see that they are not there accidentally or unnecessarily?

2. To whom is God calling *you* to proclaim his mystery? How might you do this?

3. Your church is a trophy cabinet of God's grace and wisdom. How will this affect your attitude about going to church next Sunday?

6. GRASPING THE SCALE OF GOD'S LOVE

When someone who loves you moves in, two marvellous things happen: they start changing everything to reflect their character, and they fill the place with their love for you! At least that's what happened when I got married, and I don't think my experience was unusual. So tatty furniture gets replaced, filthy rugs get cleaned and curtains finally get hung. Even more radical alterations, like taking down the poster of your favourite rugby team and the introduction of countless fluffy cushions, seem tolerable when you feel loved!

And this is the ongoing experience of every Christian. When the Spirit of Christ takes up residence in our lives, he redecorates our souls with his holy character. And he fills our hearts with more and more of his love. And I seriously doubt whether many of us have realised quite how much Jesus Christ loves us. Let's invite the apostle Paul to explain as he shares with us another of his prayers.

Kneeling Before the Father

In **verse 14** Paul resumes his letter from where he broke off in verse 1: "For this reason I kneel before the Father". He has now clarified at least three motivations that give him reason to pray for his readers again:

His first reason for prayer is the wonder of God's eternal plan, which is the subject of his whole letter, "to bring unity to all things in heaven and on earth under Christ" (1:10). This plan has now been greatly enriched by his explanation of his own ministry (3:2-13), of proclaiming to the Gentiles the "boundless riches of Christ" (v 8) in the "mystery of Christ" (v 4)—the gospel that Jew and Gentile alike can be saved in Christ. And all this so that now, "through the church, the manifold wisdom of God [in gathering sinners under Christ through his death] should be made known to the rulers and authorities in the heavenly realms" (3:10)—demonstrating his conquest of evil in the spiritual realms. This epic plan provides good reason for Paul to pray that his readers will rejoice in God's unfolding plan.

Paul's second reason for prayer is that, when he broke off his line of thinking in 3:1, he'd just finished explaining how God's eternal plan to reconcile everything under Christ is being accomplished in two dimensions of vertical reconciliation with God (2:1-10) and horizontal reconciliation with others in the church (2:11-22). This double reconciliation gives Paul added reason to pray that the Ephesians will appreciate the death and resurrection of Christ for their peace with God and with each other.

The third reason for Paul's prayer is the specific encouragement he had offered just before he broke off in 2:22: "In him you too are being built together to become a dwelling in which God lives by his Spirit". This is a privilege and responsibility that he prays about, and will shortly amplify, in this passage.

Notice how Paul prays for such big things to be accomplished in his readers' lives. Our heavenly Father is certainly concerned about the smallest details of our daily needs, but sometimes we can use this as an excuse to childishly focus our prayers upon selfish or trivial things. In our Bible studies, we can easily read magnificent passages like this and then close the Bible just to pray about a weekend barbecue and the children's colds! If we could learn to pray not only for our daily needs but also for God's big spiritual plans for other people which are described in the passage, we would be more likely to witness God answering our prayers. The truth is that God cares much more about my son becoming a fit dwelling for the Holy Spirit than about what score he gets in his science test!

The Father and the Family

And look who Paul is conscious of praying to: "the Father, from whom every family [all fatherhood] in heaven and on earth derives its name" (**3:14-15**). Paul kneels in surrendered reverence to our loving heavenly Father, who provides and enables many kinds of family, which reflect the "family" of the **Trinity**. These include his family of angels in heaven, his families of every culture around the world (created by God as the basic loving community of our societies for nurturing children to love him), and especially his local church families of adopted children everywhere. Families are not an accident of **social evolution** that can be dispensed with. Families, however dysfunctional they are because of sin, are a reflection of the family of our trinitarian God, who is Father, Son and Holy Spirit. Indeed, churches often need to provide the kind of family support that our natural families haven't because they've been so damaged by abuse, alcoholism or jealousy. Churches can be a family for those in need because of serious illness, bereavement, unemployment, homelessness, etc. Indeed, when we face suffering, our heavenly Father commonly doesn't remove us from the sufferings of this world, but sends members of our church family into our suffering to help us.

> Our Father commonly doesn't remove us *from* suffering, but sends members of our church family *into* our suffering.

So Paul kneels in prayer to Almighty God as "Our Father..." We easily forget how stunning it is to call the supreme Being, the Creator and Governor of the universe, "Father". The Aramaic word, *Abba*, which Jesus used, means "Dad" (affectionate but respectful). No human religion or Jewish teacher ever dared to call God "Dad". Jesus knew that the first principle of prayer, and the rocket engine that drives us to pray, is not technique but theology—understanding not *how* to pray but *who* we pray to. Indeed, his recommended opening,

"Our Father in heaven" (Matthew 6:9), summarises the entire gospel work of Christ—that we may enjoy "adoption to sonship through Jesus Christ" (Ephesians 1:5)—which is the miracle of grace and the basis of prayer. As adopted children, we are entitled to speak to "Our Father" in the name of his Son in the power of his Spirit, knowing that he's more powerful and loving and wise than any earthly father, or anyone else we might turn to in a crisis.

Our heavenly Father loves us passionately and perfectly. Unlike human fathers he's always available, always knows what's best (for us to become more like Jesus), is always patient and kind, and is always able to provide whatever is necessary. He is generous but wise, firm in discipline but quick to forgive; he never breaks a promise and he goes with us everywhere. He's truly the best Father anyone could want, especially for those who've had dreadful or absent human fathers.

But what is it that Paul asks the Father to give his children? You may be surprised to realise that three times he asks for "power" (**3:16, 18, 20**)! We're often anxious about asking for power—perhaps for fear of becoming like "prosperity" preachers on television, who exploit the naïve by offering power to get rich or get healed—to whoever has enough misguided faith to send them money. That is not the "power" Paul is praying for; he is asking for "power through [God's] Spirit in your inner being, so that Christ may dwell in your hearts" (**v 16-17**); "power ... to grasp" or comprehend (**v 18**); and "his power that is at work within us" (**v 20**).

Power to Welcome Christ

In essence, Paul is praying in **3:16-17** that these believers would have power to welcome Christ into our hearts. Let's unpack these glorious phrases:

- "... out of his glorious riches" (**v 16**) means that the origin of the power that the Ephesians need will always be the inexhaustible riches of God's glory. As we make efforts to change our affections and behaviours, it will only be by his power that we can change in deep and lasting ways; for example, that...

- ■ "... he may strengthen you with power through his Spirit in your inner being" (**v 16**), which means that their power will not be a visible or obvious strength to parade around, but the invisible power of spiritual convictions created by the Holy Spirit in their hearts, in order that...

- ■ "... Christ may dwell in your hearts through faith" (**v 17**), which means that Christ will, as we would say, "make himself at home" in their hearts. This seems strange because Paul has already said in 1:13-14 that all Christians, having believed, are "marked in him with a seal, the promised Holy Spirit, who is a deposit guaranteeing our inheritance until the **redemption** of those who are God's possession". Clearly, the Holy Spirit lives in us from the moment we believe the gospel of Christ. But the word "dwell" here in **3:17** doesn't just mean to arrive, but to settle down. Paul is not praying that the Holy Spirit of Christ will come upon them, but that he would make himself at home in their hearts, at the centre of their affections, decisions and behaviour.

Notice how the strengthening of the Spirit is parallel with the indwelling of Christ—it is by the power of God's Holy Spirit indwelling us that Christ Jesus in heaven is present in us, transforming us from the inside.

This strengthening presence is experienced "through faith" (**v 17**). This does not mean that if we invent enough belief, then it will seem to happen, nor that if we have enough determination, we will twist God's arm to make him do what we want. No, it means that through the Bible, the Holy Spirit strengthens our personal trust in the Christ we meet there, so we get to know him better. For faith is not just an initial reliance upon Christ for salvation. It continues as a daily personal relationship of confidence in Christ—as our Saviour, who keeps us forgiven and safe, and as our Lord, who guides us and provides for us daily. The Holy Spirit loves to strengthen this personal faith through his word.

This is what we might call the Spirit's "floodlight ministry". I once saw a wonderful sound and light show at the "Blue Mosque" in

Istanbul. An incredible array of spotlights lit up the magnificent main dome, six minarets and eight minor domes. The spotlights were not there to draw attention to themselves, but to highlight the magnificence of the building. Likewise, the ministry of the Holy Spirit is to draw attention to the magnificence of Jesus, rather than to himself. Churches and individuals in whom Jesus is continually glorified and loved are churches and individuals that are full of the Holy Spirit.

Spiritual Renovation

And a person in whom the Spirit is working powerfully is someone who will be changing deeply. When the Spirit of Christ makes himself at home, he constantly renovates our hearts to make us a more appropriate dwelling for the Lord Jesus, because the Lord Jesus is not merely dropping in briefly. He is staying for ever. When someone comes for a short visit, they usually just leave their stuff in their travel bags and try not to disturb the room. But when someone moves into a new home permanently, they change the wallpaper, paint the ceiling, replace the carpet and chuck out the old furniture. When the Spirit of Christ moves in, he gradually redecorates everywhere. Room by room, the horrible old wallpapers of selfishness are replaced with a brand new wallpaper called love; the old ceilings darkened by fear of death are repainted with bright colours of hope in the resurrection of Christ; filthy old carpets stained by years of immorality are replaced with clean new carpets of purity and kindness; and the rickety old furniture of idolatry is gradually replaced with sparkling new ministries that worship Jesus.

As a newly married couple must learn to live together by discussing and taking decisions together, so a Christian will want to know Christ's opinion in the Bible about the decisions they make together every day. We learn to pray—for discernment to apply the principles of God's word to our options, for wisdom to make godly choices, and for God's sovereign will to govern the outcome.

And as newly married couples replace selfish pursuits with joint enterprise, so Christians empowered by the indwelling Spirit of Christ will gradually kill off ("mortify") self-indulgence and take up the service of others. And as we make changes together, Christ will feel more "at home" in our lives. This is why Paul prays for power: not for the Ephesians to become successful and famous, but to become godly and clean—with renovated hearts. There's a lot to be changed for our distinguished new resident. But the great thing is that, even when we rebel and fail—like annoying flatmates who play their music too loud, or thoughtless husbands who leave their dirty clothes lying around— our Lord will never walk out on us. We're now his home address. It won't always be easy—he loves us too much to do nothing about our sin. He will gently and gradually but radically be transforming our interior—because he loves us.

> We are now Christ's home address. And he will radically reform our interior.

It's been my joy over the last twenty years as Senior Pastor of our church to watch people being converted by the Spirit of Christ through the word of God. I was once invited by a local gathering of **liberal** clergy to explain why our church had been growing steadily all these years, when their churches were declining. They wanted to know what management strategy we employ to get people to serve so willingly and give money and time so generously. I kept explaining that we keep carefully expounding the Scriptures but they didn't want hear about that. "How are you attracting so many young people? How do you raise up leaders? How are you raising your finance? What is your vision-selling technique and your team-building tactic? What strategy are you using to recruit your church-planting teams? Why do so many men come to your church?" they asked. I tried to explain that all these things were the natural product of people being continually converted and trained by the Spirit of God through the word of God. The power for growth and change was the Holy Spirit of Christ giving people new birth, taking up residence in them, and gradually transforming them into godly, generous, gospel ministers. But they didn't want to hear what this passage says, because they didn't want to focus upon Bible-teaching. If we do, we will pray like Paul for the power of God's Spirit to welcome Christ to renovate our hearts as we surrender our hearts to his transforming words in Scripture.

Questions for reflection

1. In times of difficulty, is your heavenly Father the first person you turn to, or the last resort when all else fails?

2. How have you experienced the Spirit's power renovating your heart as a home fit for Christ?

3. How have these verses encouraged you to pray, and helped you to know what to pray for?

PART TWO

Power to Appreciate

In **verse 17**, Paul employs an organic, botanical metaphor to explain what else he prays for the Ephesians: "And I pray that you, being rooted and established in love..." The self-sacrificial love of God in Christ, revealed most clearly at the cross and experienced in every facet of our relationship with him, is like the soil in which a beautiful shrub can grow. It's the nutrient that our faith needs to flourish and bloom. We experience human love not only in episodes of ecstatic passion, but also in sustained and patient support over time. Likewise, we experience Christ's love not only in exciting episodes when we are overcome by his love on the cross, but also in his sustained practical and spiritual support and encouragements over many years. In this personal relationship with God, Paul prays that the Ephesians will appreciate and know, not just intellectually but with the whole of their being, the vast scale of his love. This recognition is, again, only possible by God's power, and not our own unaided effort.

It is striking that God's power enabling us to grasp his love is most effective when we reflect on the gospel "together with all the Lord's holy people" (**v 18**). We can't easily fathom his love on our own. For instance, as our church is currently celebrating our Silver Jubilee of twenty-five years of God's kindness, it has become obvious that none of us are special on our own; but as a church family, we have witnessed the remarkable kindness of our Lord in countless wonderful ways.

We will need the Spirit's work in the company of other Christians "to grasp how wide and long and high and deep is the love of Christ" (**v 18**). It's best to interpret this remarkable phrase in the context of other Bible passages that use the dimensions of the cosmos or the earth or the temple to exalt the immeasurable greatness and goodness of God (eg: "For as high as the heavens are above the earth, so great is his love for those who fear him; as far as the east is from the west, so far has he removed our transgressions from us", Psalm 103:11-12).

Moreover, Paul here invents dimensions which are remarkably appropriate to the major themes of this letter concerning God's grace. Consider each of the following dimensions in Ephesians **3:18** as we seek to grasp how massively Christ is in love with us:

- ■ "Wide" illustrates his *accepting* love. Paul has already celebrated how the love of Christ embraces Jew and Gentile and anyone from any background who comes to him for mercy: "He came and preached peace to you who were far away and peace to those who were near" (2:17). Perhaps some of us are tempted to feel that we're beyond the reach of his love—that our background is too immoral, or too poor, or too privileged, or too idolatrous, or too dysfunctional for us to be genuinely loved by Jesus. We need God's help to grasp how wide the love of Christ is. If you are trusting in Christ, there is nothing you have done or could ever do that would put you outside his embrace. His is a wide and accepting love.

- ■ "Long" illustrates his *lasting* love. Paul has already celebrated the eternity of God's love from before the foundation of the world to the eternal future forever: "In love he predestined us for adoption to sonship through Jesus Christ" (1:4-5). Perhaps some of us have been painfully abandoned in the past by someone who promised to love us—a father, a husband or a girlfriend. The world is full of people who say "I love you", but don't mean it. Or perhaps we worry that he'll give up on us because we're just not changing enough, and we suspect he'll get fed up with our constant failures. We need to grasp that his love for us is permanent. However badly and however often we disappoint him, he will never let us go. He has committed himself to love us from eternity past for eternity everlasting and will never, ever, ever, give up on us. His is a long and lasting love!

- ■ "High" illustrates his *exalting* love. Paul has also celebrated how the love of God in Christ does not simply save us from hell, but lifts us high into heaven: "God raised us up with Christ and seated us with him in the heavenly realms in Christ Jesus, in order that in the coming ages he might show the incomparable riches of his grace, expressed in his kindness to us in Christ Jesus" (2:6-7). Perhaps you sometimes wonder whether it is really worth being a Christian, and whether Christ really has much to offer, or whether the benefits will ever outweigh the heavy costs. We need to grasp how high is the love of Christ, how much he has in store for us in eternity, and how exalted and privileged we shall be for ever in the new creation. Christ's love has lifted us from the gutter to this palace, from hell to heaven. His is a high and exalting love.

We need to grasp how much Christ has in store for us in eternity.

- "Deep" illustrates his *sacrificial* love. Paul has already celebrated the self-sacrifice of Christ for our sins on the cross: "In him we have redemption through his blood, the forgiveness of sins, in accordance with the riches of God's grace that he lavished on us" (1:7-8). Have you ever really considered the depths of the agony of Christ in suffering not only the physical tortures of beatings and crucifixion, and the public humiliation of being strung up naked as a criminal to be mocked and abused, but also the spiritual trauma of suffering in his own soul the hell that all his people deserve? Have you stopped recently to realise that he accepted such depths of agony out of personal love for you? Perhaps some of us think that the things we've done, or repeatedly done, in a red-light district or on a battlefield or in the office or on the internet or in our imagination are too terrible to be forgiven. We need to grasp that Jesus Christ not only knows the filthy things that we've done, and the far more numerous kind things that we completely failed to even consider doing, but he willingly accepted deep into his soul all the punishments that we deserve. His is an incredibly deep, sacrificial love!

It is sadly normal for people to seriously underestimate the scale of the love of Christ. It's easy for us Christians to forget how massively loved we are with such a wide and accepting, long and lasting, high and exalting, deep and sacrificial love. And tragically, unbelievers are often completely unaware of how loving God is. Atheists like Richard Dawkins and Stephen Fry accuse God of being a cruel monster; they seem to be blind to the love of God.

In 2009, the *Daily Mirror* British newspaper published the story of Bombardier Robert Key, who died in World War II when a grenade he was holding exploded. An army report blamed him for "showing off" with the grenade in the recaptured French town of Annezin in September 1944. His family were apparently ashamed because his service record cited "foolish" behaviour for his death, and they refused to talk about him for 65 years. But when the town's mayor traced Robert's family in Coventry in 2008, to ask permission to name a road after Robert, the truth began to emerge. The family discovered that Robert had in fact snatched the grenade from a large group of children he'd found playing with it. When one boy pulled out the pin, Bombardier Key seized the grenade and fled away, clutching the grenade to his stomach to protect the children when it exploded. To this day, Robert remains a legend in the town of Annezin. Robert's nephew, Robert Furber, 62, said: "This news was amazing and completely different to anything we'd known". For unbelievers and, to some degree, believers, the sheer scale of the love of Christ is "completely different to anything we'd known".

Know the Unknowable

Paul isn't content that his readers are just "rooted and established in love" (**3:17**) when they initially became Christians—nor just that they "grasp" the theology of the dimensions of the love of Christ in their heads (**v 18**). He wants them to "know this love that surpasses knowledge" (**v 19**).

He's saying that although the love of Christ is too big to ever fully comprehend, Christians can live in the knowledge of his love, even though we'll always feel out of our depth. By way of illustration, the deepest part of the ocean known to scientists is the Challenger Deep Gorge in the great Mariana Trench in the north-west Pacific Ocean. It is seven miles deep, a mile deeper than Mount Everest is tall. There is no submersible currently able to survive the crushing pressures at the bottom to explore it. But even though we can't plumb the depths of the ocean to fully comprehend it, we still want to enjoy swimming in it and not just stand on the beach analysing it—to play in the surf off the Cornish coast, or dive down to marvel at the tropical fish of the Great Barrier Reef or bathe in the sun-kissed waters of the Caribbean. Likewise, Paul wants his readers to dwell prayerfully on the vast dimensions of Christ's love and then to live daily in the reassurance of it; so that despite the shame of our sin, the hostility of the world and the lies of the evil one, we remain confident in the gospel, swimming in the bottomless ocean of Christ's love, ever exploring more of the unknowable. It takes God's power to live by such confident faith in the love of Christ, so like Paul, we need to pray for it—for others as well as ourselves.

And as God deepens our knowledge of his measureless love, we will gradually be "filled to the measure of all the fullness of God" (**v 19**). Paul has already described the church as "[Christ's] body, the fullness of him who fills everything in every way" (1:23). Now he is speaking of personally experiencing what is readily available to us all in his church. Much as a newly married wife may intellectually grasp the concept that her new husband loves her, she will only really know that love when she experiences being loved in a thousand little ways over many years that gradually fill her life with him. So also with Christ. He is fully ours from the moment he calls us to himself. But we are being gradually filled with his Spirit (5:18), as Paul explains in a parallel passage, as we "let the word of Christ dwell in [us] richly" (Colossians 3:16, ESV), as we reflect upon a thousand little expressions of Christ's accepting, lasting, exalting and sacrificial love by his Spirit in his word, focused where "X marks the spot"—at the cross.

But how can we realistically make progress in becoming a suitable dwelling for Christ, the King of kings? And how can we ever really know this unknowable love of Christ? Has Paul gone too far? Has he asked for too much? Not when we realise the power of the God to whom he has prayed and to whom we still pray, "who is able to do immeasurably more than all we ask or imagine, according to his power that is at work within us" (Ephesians **3:20**). God is able to act immeasurably (literally "super-abundantly") beyond all we can ask or even imagine—and I can imagine a great deal! That immense power is within us to change us and use us for his glory. No one is too tough for his transforming power.

For two decades at our church, at every one of our monthly "central prayer meetings", we have finished our time of prayer by reading out loud these words from **verses 20-21**. We use them to remind each other of the greatness of the One to whom we have prayed.

> We're tempted to think that God means well and wants the best, but can't really change things.

So often, we're tempted to think that God means well, and wants the best, but can't really change things. So we feel reluctant to pray with confidence. But when we ask for things that will further his plan to bring all things together under Christ, including helping us to become a fitting home for his Spirit and to know the unknowable love of Christ, we need to remember who we're talking to. God is willing and able to do immeasurably more for us and in us than anyone could ever imagine, because he loves his ordinary churches with an immeasurably gigantic love. And the more we experience his patient, transforming love, the more we will cry out with Paul in joy: "To him be glory in the church and in Christ Jesus throughout all generations, for ever and ever! Amen" (**v 21**).

Questions for reflection

1. Reflect on a time when you struggled as a Christian, or repeatedly gave in to a particular sin. How was that connected with a failure to grasp Christ's love for you?

2. Wide... long... high... deep... Which aspect of Christ's love particularly thrills you today?

3. If you truly believe verses 20-21, what difference will it make to your prayer life?

7. HOW CHURCHES GROW

How do churches grow?

This isn't just an important question for church-planting movements or for churches with a particular taste for mission. It's a vital question for all churches and all the members of churches; because we've learned from Ephesians that God's eternal plan is "to bring unity to all things in heaven and on earth under Christ" (1:10), in which his triumphant centrepiece is his church, so that "through the church, the manifold wisdom of God should be made known to the rulers and authorities in the heavenly realms" (3:10). God wants his heavenly church to display in the spiritual realms the triumphant wisdom of his character and plans, revealed and accomplished in the astonishing death and resurrection of Christ. This happens as his earthly congregations continue gathering people from all nations under the rule of Christ to share in his holiness.

All churches should therefore be trying to grow in number and in holiness—growth glorifies God. We need to avoid separating the holiness of a church from its mission of making disciples. For, as the holiness of God is expressed in the loving gathering of his own Trinity, so his grace to mankind is expressed in the evangelistic gathering of his church. Church growth is not a secondary priority—Ephesians teaches us that gathering people under Christ is central to the purpose of churches, because it displays the wisdom of God. Growth glorifies God!

But what does God want us to do to generate this growth? We can learn from numerous church-growth studies. Lots of them talk about providing a compelling vision, inspiring leadership, a committed membership, self-reflecting humility, flexible structures and so on. Such recommendations seem eminently sensible, but many of these principles would grow a business as well as a church. Indeed, some mega-churches out there have grown into massive organisations with huge buildings and enormous financial resources, but have precious little to do with the gospel of Christ crucified. Numerical and economic growth do not necessarily represent spiritual church growth. What must we do to ensure the spiritual expansion of our churches through numerical growth of God-exalting holy disciples of Christ?

We can certainly learn from other churches that have grown spiritually. For example, many have learned from the evangelistic strategies of community outreach established under the leadership of John Stott at All Souls Langham Place, London, and many of us use the excellent *Christianity Explored* evangelistic materials developed there. Many churches have learned from the focus upon sustained, expository Bible-preaching modelled by Dick Lucas at St Helen's Bishopsgate, London, and are convinced of the value of high-quality Bible-study groups and one-to-one Bible-reading developed by the team there. Many churches have also learned from the commitment to training up gospel workers developed by Phillip Jensen at St. Matthias in Sydney, and look to recruit "apprentices" in gospel ministry for the next generation. And many churches have both learned from the strategic thinking of Tim Keller at Redeemer Church, Manhattan, and from the clear organisational thinking of Andrew Heard at EV Church in New South Wales, Australia, and are convinced of the need to plant churches that develop a clear gospel vision for reaching their community before choosing which kinds of ministry to invest in.

But we shouldn't *blindly* copy the patterns of ministry at such city-centre churches; their contexts, resources and history may be very different from those of our own churches.

We can also learn from our own experience. It's never a good idea to uncritically import models of ministry from alien contexts—it's important to apply biblical principles to our own circumstances and reflectively learn how to practise them excellently. But what are those biblical principles? God doesn't reveal his ways in history, whether our own history or the history of others, but in his word. So what are the biblical church-growth principles that need to form the core of our church-gathering ministries?

The Fundamentals

In Ephesians 4, Paul explicitly outlines the fundamental principles of how God grows churches in all times and all places. Remember that Paul's letter to the Ephesians is a game of two halves. Chapters 1 – 3 have celebrated God's eternal plan: to gather all things in heaven and on earth together under Christ (chapter 1), through the death and resurrection of Christ, which reconciles us to God and to each other (chapter 2), to manifest the triumphant wisdom of his gospel mystery to the spiritual realms in his church (chapter 3). Now, in chapters 4 – 6, Paul is explaining how his readers must live as a church committed to gathering people under Christ. He outlines three basic ingredients for church growth here in **4:1-16**.

These fundamental principles of genuine spiritual growth are the same for every church in every context. There's nothing weird or complicated here. The prayerful and careful application of these principles will take time and sacrifice, but this is how God always grows his churches. The three themes clarified here are, simply, **unity** in **ministry** for **maturity**. This is how God gathers people into churches under Christ!

Maintaining Unity

Paul is concerned for a deep unity in every local church that reflects the unity we've already been given in the heavenly church, for the "calling" received by every Christian from God through his gospel (**v 1**) is not only into Christ, but also into the unity of his church. In **verses 2-6**, he's not concerned with co-operation between churches scattered throughout the world such as we enjoy in all kinds of wider "para-church" co-operation (whether global missions, national denominations, regional partnerships, or local church-planting networks). These are the wonderful collaborative efforts of God's scattered people partnering in the work of extending God's kingdom (by calling all nations through the gospel to surrender to the rule of the King) and requiring different degrees of theological agreement depending on the kind of ministry being shared. But Paul is concerned here with relational unity in the gospel *within* churches. He outlines three attitudes crucial for accomplishing such unity, followed by seven wonderful motives for pursuing it.

The three attitudes to nourish are humility, gentleness and patience. Paul tells us first to be "humble" (**v 2**). Being "humble" is not being shy. It means restraining our sense of entitlement to be the focus of other people's care and attention, by submitting ourselves to others with respect, in order to promote their best interests, eg: allowing someone else's teaching or musical talents to be more celebrated in our church than our own, or in realising that our desire for attention from a leader may need to remain neglected while they are pressured with caring for others (who may be facing desperate crises that we know little about). In the words of an oft-quote paraphrase of C.S. Lewis' observations in *Mere Christianity*:

> Being gentle means dealing with others with kindness rather than roughness.

"Humility is not thinking less of yourself; it's thinking of yourself less."

Next, being "gentle" (literally "meek") is not being weak. It means dealing with other people with kindness rather than roughness, with empathetic compassion rather than demanding force, and with soft encouragement rather than hard bullying—for instance, urging people to raise their standards for Jesus' sake by setting a good example rather than cajoling them to adopt our own agenda by being demanding or critical.

Third, to be "patient" means to be longsuffering of the faults of others and slow in seeking to rebuke them, recognising that spiritual growth takes time and that we are all work in progress. We are called to be patient, for instance, when those who are younger in faith seem unreliable or lazy; or when we experience less love than we have tried to show to others.

These attitudes are probably especially challenging for those of us from the more privileged, "sharp-elbowed" middle classes. Our up-bringing may mean that we don't struggle so much with violence, theft or promiscuity, but find humility, gentleness and patience very difficult indeed. This is because our Western culture indulges our self-promoting view that being opinionated, aggressive and ambitious for ourselves and our families is a good thing. But such arrogance is really a sin that strangles the growth of a church, because we end up pulling our church in different directions.

By contrast, our Lord Jesus was famously humble, gentle and pa-tient with everyone he met, and has been incredibly humble, gentle and patient in dealing with us! Obeying Paul's words here really means growing more like Jesus. It can happen as we seek the Spirit's help to recognise and repent of the selfishness that was perhaps indulged in our upbringing, of those poisonous influences of Western education encouraging self-promotion and attention-seeking, and of the pride of our hearts, which makes us demanding and consumerist. In our conversations, we could try to enquire humbly after other people's tri-umphs and troubles before telling them about our own. Before church meetings we could resolve to gently allow others to have the first say and the last word. At our church gatherings, we could try to rejoice patiently in seeing others welcomed and cared for instead of asserting our own needs.

Growing in Christ-like humility, gentleness and patience will enable us gradually to achieve Paul's twin aims for church communities: first, "bearing with one another in love" (**v 2**) means accepting the fail-ures and flaws of others because we love them; and second, making "every effort to keep the unity of the Spirit through the bond of peace" (**v 3**) means protecting the "unity of the Spirit", which is the special togetherness that the Holy Spirit creates in a congregation. This is our shared experience of adoption into God's family for peace with God and peace with each other in Christ. We are to do everything we possibly can, in whatever roles we have, to pursue and maintain the unity of our church in Christ instead of fuelling division. When tension arises, as it occasionally will in every church family, rather than stirring things up with over-confident opinions, destructive gossip or bitter aggression, we are prayerfully to encourage and help each other to listen humbly, speak gently and forgive patiently.

One...

As Paul now explains, God has already given us a very special spiritual unity in Christ, unlike anything else in society, which provides multiple motivations to congregational co-operation. Seven are listed here: "There is one body and one Spirit, just as you were called to one hope when you were called; one Lord, one faith, one baptism; one God and Father of all, who is over all and through all and in all" (**v 4-6**). Paul is describing the unity that each of the three persons within the Godhead creates between Christians in God's church:

- One "Spirit" has called us into the one "body" of the church through the one "hope" of eternal life in the gospel of Christ (**v 4**).

- One "Lord", Jesus, is proclaimed in the one gospel "faith" of Scripture, symbolised in our shared "baptism" (literally "soaking") in the Holy Spirit when we were born again (represented in the ceremony of baptism that symbolises this cleansing in Christ) (**v 5**).

- One "God and Father" is the origin, ruler and sustaining presence of everything and everyone in the universe (**v 6**).

Since God is himself a unity of persons who are different but equal and ordered in love for each other, every church he gathers under Christ is to be a unity of different but equal persons ordered in sacrificially loving roles, serving each other. How exciting to realise that our church community reflects our Creator!

In this sense, each local church is like a symphony orchestra. The different musicians skilfully combine their talents to make beautiful music. But imagine if the string section becomes competitive and starts showing off by playing faster than everyone else, so the brass section gets aggressive and plays so loudly that they totally dominate and you can't hear anyone else. Then the wind section gets so upset with all the conflict that they stop playing entirely, and the percussion section overreacts and starts throwing their drumsticks at the rest of the orchestra! Their music would sound dreadful and the conductor would have to rebuke them, or the audience would quickly leave.

In fact that is what has often happened—not in orchestras, but in churches. Too often, God's people have been characterised by self-centredness, sharp tongues and an appetite for conflict. People have left their local church never to return, and others have simply steered well clear. And God has not been glorified in the heavenly realms!

A squabbling orchestra would surely be told: "Stop this squabbling—you're incredibly privileged to have been chosen and assembled in this orchestra to play Mozart's beautiful music. Now play nicely!" And the apostle Paul wants to remind us: *Stop arguing—you're incredibly privileged to have been chosen and gathered into your local church to co-operate in God's stunningly beautiful plan to gather people under Christ. So be humble, gentle and patient, and play nicely!*

> Churches can be damaged by being too soft or by being too *hard*.

We are elsewhere required to "contend" (ie: fight) for the apostolic faith of the Bible against those "who pervert the grace of our God into a licence for immorality" (Jude v 4). Sadly, many leaders in established Western denominations are perverting the gospel and need to be challenged to believe and teach, and appoint others who will only teach, the gospel-driven holiness of Christ in the Scriptures. But Paul writes elsewhere: "Don't have anything to do with foolish and stupid arguments, because you know they produce quarrels. And the Lord's servant must not be quarrelsome" (2 Timothy 2:23-24). So within our churches, in the way we behave towards other people, so far as depends upon us, we must seek to live at peace, showing patient tolerance towards everyone. Churches can be damaged either by being too soft—when we should be courageously contending for the gospel with false teachers—or by being too hard—when we should be more patiently tolerant with our brothers and sisters in Christ. The wisdom to discern the difference, which God intends us to display in the spiritual realms, comes from rejoicing in people from a diversity of cultures gathering into the unity of one gospel faith.

Questions for reflection

1. How can you proactively help to maintain unity in your church?

2. Who do you find it hard to act patiently towards? How can a deep love of the gospel enable you to remain loving towards that person?

3. How well is your church reaching, welcoming and uniting people of diverse backgrounds? How might you contribute to these efforts?

PART TWO

Contribute Your Ministry

Having emphasised the importance of unity in Christ's body for spiritual growth, Paul now explains the value of diverse ministries among its members: "But to each one of us grace has been given as Christ apportioned it" (Ephesians **4:7**). Every single believer in Christ, without exception, has been given some "grace". Paul is not referring here to God saving us by grace alone in Christ dying for us, but to his subsequent additional grace in giving us gifts of ministry as Christ has distributed them. These are given not for our personal satisfaction or reputation, but to enrich the life and service of others in our church. These gifts of grace are not just abilities but ministries—ways for us to serve his church family.

As Paul explains more fully elsewhere (for instance in 1 Corinthians 12 and Romans 12), this means that none of us should indulge any feelings of inadequacy, for we all have something to contribute. Indeed, the church will be weakened if we don't offer our ministry. And none of us should indulge feelings of superiority, because none of us have all the gifts. Indeed, we will eventually discover that we all need the ministries of other people in our church. This diversity of ministries in a church is something to be celebrated and enjoyed, however frustrating our cultural and personality differences may sometimes feel.

Moreover, since Christ apportions the gifts, there's no point in feeling envious of someone else's gift or proud of our own. For Christ has decided how to apportion them. We're approved of, and rewarded in heaven, by God for our godliness rather than our giftedness. Whether we serve others by praying for them, reading the Bible with them or encouraging them, by serving on a coffee or stewarding rota or

> We're approved of by God for our godliness rather than our giftedness.

in a children's ministry or Bible-study group, Paul wants to emphasise where these gifts of ministry come from.

This is why he follows up the great truth of Ephesians **4:7** by quoting from Psalm 68. This is initially difficult to interpret. But Paul is simply emphasising that the risen Christ has not only saved us but has entrusted each of us with gifts for our church. When "he ascended on high, he took many captives and gave gifts to his people" (Ephesians **4:8**). The psalm originally celebrated the victory of God in rescuing Israel from Egypt and then giving his redeemed people back to the world. Paul recognises that this psalm looked forward to the victory of Christ in ascending to heaven (**v 10**)—after descending into this world to die for us (**v 9**)—and in then giving us all back as gifts to his churches. We don't just have God's gifts. We are God's gifts to his church. So my church is not just there in order to bless me, as though I am a shopper filling my basket in the supermarket. The opposite is true: we're all saved and given to our churches as gifts to bless others by serving them. We are not meant to be consumers but contributors!

Equipped to Equip

But how can we be that? Paul explains that Jesus has given his church apostles, prophets, evangelists, pastors and teachers (**v 11**) "to equip his people for works of service, so that the body of Christ may be built up" (**v 12**).

Paul has already referred to the apostles and prophets, who were, together with Christ the cornerstone, the foundation of the church that Christ is building (2:20). So here, it seems he is saying that Jesus has given us a series of different kinds of Bible teachers—beginning with the foundational apostles, who were appointed by Christ as his witnesses and empowered by his Spirit to write the New Testament, together with the original first-century prophets (as in 2:20 he is probably not speaking here about the prophecy of all Christians in evangelism and biblical insight), who taught and preserved the faith until the New Testament was completed; now Christ continues to provide us with evangelists, who bring people to Christ and train others to do so; and pastor-teachers (Paul probably has one role in mind here), who build us up in Christ by nurturing our faith.

But we are not to merely be "receivers". Teachers of every kind in the church have been given by Jesus to "equip his people for works of service" (this word can also be translated "ministry" or "worship")— to equip all of us for our many different ministries that will grow and build up the church, to glorify God.

So all of us have ministries and we are all ministers; and we are all being equipped by our Bible-teachers for our particular church-growth ministries!

> Churches can be like a soccer match: 22,000 spectators in need of exercise and 22 players in need of a rest.

This means that our church needs us all to get involved, and not leave the ministry to a few! It has been said that churches can be like a soccer match: 22,000 spectators desperately in need of some exercise and 22 players desperately in need of a rest! Indeed, if we compare Sunday church to a football match, many people think of church as like a crowd of spectators (the congregation) gathering to watch expensive professional players (the pastors) playing the game (doing their ministry of preaching and leading meetings, etc).

But Paul says that Bible teachers are given by Jesus "to equip his people for works of service, so that the body of Christ may be built up" (**v 12**). It is the works of "service" ("ministry") of God's people in the congregation that builds up the church in unity and maturity. It's not just the Bible teachers who do ministry. The whole congregation are the ministers that Jesus employs to build his church. To continue the soccer **analogy**, if our church was a soccer club (let's call it "Church United FC"), the players on the pitch would be the congregations. Their Bible teachers are player-coaches, training them to play the game of loving God, loving each other and loving their community, working as a team against the world, the flesh and the devil. The spectators are the watching world of unbelieving friends, family, work colleagues and local community:

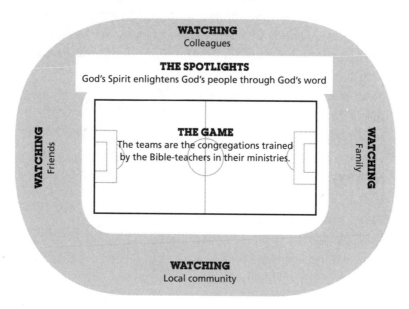

This understanding profoundly affects the way we "do church". The Bible teachers, whether employed staff or **lay** leaders, are not the only "ministers". They are training all the congregation in ministry. Our "ministry teams" should therefore be huge, involving every church member! All our churches should be "training churches", and all our members ministers, because that is how Jesus builds his church.

Grow in Maturity

Jesus doesn't want our churches just to be united in diversity and busy with ministry; he wants them to grow up in maturity in Christ-likeness. He uses three similar phrases to describe this goal: "unity in the faith", "become mature" and "fullness of Christ" (**v 13**).

This "unity in the faith" means a shared and true understanding of God revealed in Christ as he is revealed in the Bible. None of us yet understand God perfectly, so Christ wants us all to grow in our understanding by discovering more in Scripture and changing our minds as we learn; we're not to be content with remaining childishly ignorant or content with conflicting opinions (especially about major issues), or to stubbornly cling to our alternative theories (it is possible to earnestly believe error), or to retire from a zeal for learning about God (for there is such joy in getting to know our Saviour better)—for our unity of mind in believing God's word is central to the unity of all things under Christ!

Indeed, churches should not become so collectively set in concrete in their ministries that they cannot be reformed by the Spirit though his word. Any church that never changes is either perfect (unlikely) or not listening to the Bible (likely). And churches that are listening repentantly to God's word will be constantly changing! We are to constantly seek to grow together in unity of faith until we become "mature", which means growing up spiritually and not remaining childishly undeveloped. It is all too easy to be content to be a spiritual Peter Pan, who wanted to remain forever a boy, and never grow up. It is tempting to keep clinging to childish, immature views of guidance or angels or judgment etc., rather like a grown man clutching his childhood teddy bear! Instead, says Paul, we need to grow up: to grow up in our understanding of God's word (**v 13**). Jesus doesn't want us all to become academics, but he does want us all to wrestle with grown-up questions about the application of Scripture to life, and, as we mature in understanding, to aspire to teach the faith to others in our family and church. Nothing is so thrilling as watching new believers growing in their knowledge and love of God's word.

To encourage us to do this, Paul shows us what kind of church this will create. First, we will attain "to the whole measure of the fullness of Christ" (**v 13**). Our Lord's intention is not just for us all to grow into a doctrinal unity, reciting the same creeds, but to mature in the whole character of Jesus Christ! Christian growth is growing to become more like Jesus, the perfect human.

And growing up means we "will no longer be infants, tossed back and forth by the waves, and blown here and there by every wind of teaching and by the cunning and craftiness of people in their deceitful scheming" (**v 14**). Some churches and Christians are a bit like little rowing boats on the Atlantic Ocean, pulled in every direction by the latest spiritual gale to blow across "the pond". I remember successive gusts of theological distortion blowing British churches around, like the "Toronto blessing", then the "Kansas City prophets", and then more recently the "emerging churches". We mustn't be like children going through successive crazes, first for Barbie and Ken action dolls, then hamsters or snakes, then scooters or skateboards, and then One Direction and clubbing.

Mind you, theologically conservative churches can also drift off course into an arrogant and prayerless intellectualism, or ungenerous materialism. Conversely, "Bible-lite" churches can happily wander into a childish obsession with simplicity in the name of evangelism—which fails to equip people to survive the hostility of the secular workplace or resist the temptations of the world. We all need to grow up so that "instead, speaking the truth in love, we will grow to become in every respect the mature body of him who is the head, that is, Christ. From him the whole body, joined and held together by every supporting ligament, grows and builds itself up in love, as each part does its work" (**v 15-16**).

So we are all to speak truthfully and lovingly. We are to counsel each other appropriately in how the gospel affects our lifestyles, decisions and attitudes. Indeed, the rediscovery of the importance of gospel conversations, such as we read Jesus having in the Gospels, which is being emphasised increasingly by the more responsible "biblical counselling" movements, is greatly to be welcomed. We do need to remember that Jesus and his Spirit are the "Counsellors" that people most need, that Jesus' conversations were largely evangelistic rather than concerned with parenting, and that we cannot be perfect before the new creation. But this passage emphasises that we need to encourage biblical conversation, and for some to be properly trained in biblical counselling for people with seriously dysfunctional issues is extremely important. Biblical conversations are a form of Bible teaching that helps people to mature in Christ-likeness.

However, this is not an excuse for us to say all the hard and horrible things we want to say to someone we dislike or find frustrating, nor to pull ourselves up by pulling others down. This could be a temptation for those of us with therapeutic gifts—to indulge an appetite for trying to "fix" other people, or to sit in judgement and exercise control over other people with our advice. Instead, we will want to bring people to the word of Christ for his counselling, recognising that none of us are perfect and that we are all continually in need of biblical counselling. We want our churches to provide many kinds of opportunity to lovingly discuss the spiritual truth of God's word. And this can greatly benefit our evangelism, too. Conversations about the impact of the gospel upon daily life will give us all much better traction in evangelising Western unbelievers who struggle to recognise the relevance of unapplied theological statements.

Do Your Part

Clearly, church growth needs all the limbs of the body to be united in gospel ministry, all the supporting ligaments of Bible teachers training us in our ministries, and the head of the body who is Christ directing the whole body through his word. Could you talk to your pastors or elders about what ministry you could contribute to the growth of your church? Could you to talk to them about accessing further training in your ministry? Is there any direction from the head of the body in Scripture that we know we are resisting, or are we neglecting our need for serious teaching, which is inhibiting the growth in Christ-like maturity of our church body in the unity of the faith in the spiritual realms?

Our churches will only be united in the ministries that grow our churches to maturity as "each part does its work" (**v 16**). This was powerfully illustrated for our church recently when a young man was converted. He had been raised and prayed for by his Christian family for many years but rebelled when he went to university. Friends remained faithful in love and prayer throughout the last decade. Then a church preacher arrested his attention with Jesus' words: "Stop doubting and believe" (John 20:27). A church evangelist then taught him the gospel through a *Christianity Explored* course, and read the Bible with him and a supportive friend on Sunday mornings for many weeks. Finally he has surrendered to Jesus and is putting his life in order, and now serves in another church family. In this co-operative way, Jesus has been growing his church through the ministries of many different people.

Quite simply, church growth is a team game. Or, as one church leader colourfully put it: "We're all knots in the net that God has thrown over the world!" Our churches need us to get involved and pull our weight. This passage teaches that we need to maintain our unity, contribute our ministry, and grow in our maturity. For this is how God gathers his church under Christ to display his triumph in the spiritual realms. So, don't neglect your ministry, leaving other exhausted church members to try and do it for you.

> Quite simply, church growth is a team game.

Here's the prayer that our church building has on its wall to help members remember what is expected of us by Christ. We are not trying to police their commitment, but we do want everyone to know what Christ wants from us in his church. We don't just want "members" to turn up, expecting to be served, like the members of a golf club, but "ministers", who come to church expecting to serve others. Why not pray this prayer as a private commitment to your own church family before God, and then try to keep it? No one but Jesus need know—but he's the only one who really matters because it's his church:

A JOINING-IN PRAYER

Almighty God our Heavenly Father, by your grace in Jesus Christ and in the power of your Holy Spirit, please help me to be prayerfully holy and joyfully obedient to your word and so, as a member of my church, in submission to its leadership, to:

BELIEVE and PROCLAIM the gospel that Christ is my loving Saviour and living Lord;

ATTEND regularly my Sunday congregation and appropriate mid-week small group;

CONTRIBUTE my prayer, time and talents to our church life and outreach; and

GIVE sacrificially for the gospel ministry of our church and its mission partners,

In the name of Jesus Christ my Lord, Amen.

Questions for reflection

1. Do you see your gifts as self-earned, and for your enjoyment or promotion, or as God-given, and for his people's service? Does the way you use your gifts prove the truth of your answer?

2. Do you, by personality, tend to speak truth without love or love without truth? Is there a situation into which you need to speak truth, but lovingly?

3. How are you, or might you start, doing your part for your church?

8. CHRISTIANS ARE NOT CHAMELEONS

Chameleons are an amazing species of lizard that can adapt their appearance to match their surroundings in order to stay camouflaged and invisible to predators.

Christians often live like spiritual chameleons, imitating the world around us in order to remain camouflaged and safe from spiritual predators who might criticise or hurt us.

We can usually tell if we're spiritual chameleons when unbelievers who have spent time with us are shocked to discover that we're Christians. It could be that we're just culturally very contemporary—but it's more likely that we've compromised. We may be consciously copying someone else: a popular friend, a successful colleague, an exciting celebrity or an impressive public figure. More probably, we're being influenced subconsciously, by our family background, our educational experience or by our society's media. For instance, we may have a spiritually damaging fixation with salary and status, because of our ambitious parents. Or we may have a spiritually unhealthy tendency to uncritically approve of ungodly religious opinions, because of our Western education in undiscerning tolerance and a fear of appearing "judgmental". Or if we're unhappily single or unhappily married, we may surrender to bitter self-pity and indulge our appetites for erotic fantasy, because we've accepted the lies of our media that we're all entitled to sexual pleasure, stunted without it, and free to seek it in private without censure. More often, and more dangerously, we live

as spiritual chameleons without even noticing that we're accommodating to secular morality; in which case we're not just like camouflaged chameleons—we're more like those unfortunate frogs that, as
every teenager knows from school science lessons, can be placed in an
open saucepan and slowly boiled to death without ever recognising a
change severe enough to make them jump out.

So Paul challenges all of us: "You must no longer live as the Gentiles do..." (**v 17**). He's saying: *Stop copying the world like chameleons and start imitating God.*

Put Off, Put On

Verse 17 begins "So"—meaning: in the light of what Paul has said
in chapters 1 – 3, about God gathering all things together under
Christ (chapter 1); through the death of Jesus that reconciles us to
God and to each other (chapter 2); demonstrating the triumphant
wisdom of God in the spiritual realms in our local churches (chapter
3); and also in the light of what he's said so far in chapter 4, calling us to "a life worthy of the calling you have received" (v 1), by
preserving our unity and contributing our ministry to grow in maturity. But most immediately, "so" follows verse 16, where Paul says
Christ's church body grows "as each part does its work". The obvious response is: "Paul, can you be more specific about this work?
What do you want us to do?"

It's striking that Paul isn't talking about church programmes but
about church godliness—for the gift that we are to our church is far
more about us being godly than about being able! Some churches
are full of talented people gradually destroying the church by pulling in different directions with great skill. In Revelation 2 – 3, the
risen Jesus praises the poor but faithful congregations of Smyrna and
Philadelphia far more than the sound but loveless "flagship" church
at Ephesus, or the wealthy but lukewarm church at Laodicea, because
the former testify more to the wisdom of God in the heavenly realms
by their surrender to Christ in holiness.

God is responsible for giving us whatever abilities our churches need, but he gives us responsibility for being holy with them! This passage calls us to be far more concerned about being godly than about being gifted. In summary, Paul tells his readers to *put off* their worldly way of thinking (Ephesians **4:17-19**); to be renewed to *put on* a godly way of thinking (**v 20-21**); and to become *imitators* of God in a life of sacrificial love (**v 25-32**). This is not actually a suggestion or invitation. It's the command of an apostle authorised by Christ to speak for him with authority. Paul will "insist on it in the Lord" (**v 17**). It isn't optional.

Notice that the way we live begins with how we think. The Bible consistently teaches that our minds are not neutral. Our sinful behaviour originates with our corrupted attitudes towards God. So godly behaviour must begin with a transformed mind. This transformation happens as God speaks through his word to cleanse and reorder our thinking, which then reshapes our attitudes, in order to purify and warm the affections of our hearts towards God, in order to redirect our wills and then ultimately our behaviour in following Jesus. So we must never despise or neglect the instruction and comprehension of our minds. The Spirit of God revives and changes his people by regenerating our minds through the Bible. For example, the great confession of sin and revival of Israel under **Nehemiah** came when **Ezra** read the word of God and the Levites "instructed the people in the Law ... they read from the Book of the Law of God, making it clear and giving the meaning so that the people understood what was being read" (Nehemiah 8:7-8). The same is true across Western societies today. Where the word of God is carefully taught and applied, people are being continually converted as their thinking, attitudes, affections, wills and finally behaviour are gradually transformed. Where such teaching is lacking, churches are sadly declining.

> The way we live begins with how we think. Our minds are not neutral.

We may worry that we cannot hope to learn the deep spiritual things of God. Unaided, that's true! But every Christian has the help of the Holy Spirit to grasp the meaning of the Bible. Paul tells Timothy: "Reflect on what I am saying, for the Lord will give you insight into all this" (2 Timothy 2:7). There are two halves to this statement. The first means "Think!" It is through thinking that the Lord grants his insights and we mustn't romantically imagine that he will give us understanding if we won't meditate on his word; for the blessed person is the one "whose delight is in the law of the LORD, and who meditates on his law day and night" (Psalm 1:2). So often, those with the deepest insights into Scripture are the people who have put in the longest hours of study!

Equally, the second half of 2 Timothy 2:7 means that we mustn't imagine that we can understand anything spiritual unless God reveals it to us as we meditate. That's why unconverted scholars can tell us the grammar and translate the words, but cannot grasp the spiritual significance of Scripture. This is why Christians pray before reading the Bible, asking God to reveal himself to their minds. Spiritual understanding comes from the Spirit of God as we study his word, for, "this is what we speak, not in words taught us by human wisdom but in words taught by the Spirit, explaining spiritual realities with Spirit-taught words. The person without the Spirit does not accept the things that come from the Spirit of God but considers them foolishness, and cannot understand them because they are discerned only through the Spirit" (1 Corinthians 2:13-14).

And as the Spirit instructs us, Paul says here, we'll learn to stop thinking like the world around us…

No More Worldly Thinking

The first step to not living like spiritual chameleons is to stop thinking like the ungodly: "You must no longer live as the Gentiles do, in the futility of their thinking" (Ephesians **4:17**).

As members of the new humanity united in the risen Christ, we must no longer live, as we all once did, like the Gentiles ("pagan nations") in the "futility"—or emptiness—of their thinking (**v 17**). This might be the empty worship of superstitious idolatry (for instance, religions that reverence a cow or river, or the stones of Stonehenge or the bones of dead people). Or it might be accepting the empty platitudes of popular folk religion that confidently reassures us that our deceased atheist uncle is "happily smiling down upon us" or that he "lives for ever in our hearts". These are kindly motivated sentiments—but they're still just myths. Or it may be the empty confidence that whichever God exists, he'll weigh up my good points and find that they substantially outweigh my bad points, and welcome me into heaven.

Why do people cherish such empty worship and platitudes with such confidence? Paul says it's because "they are darkened in their understanding and separated from the life of God because of the ignorance that is in them due to the hardening of their hearts" (**v 18**). Futile and empty ideas come from "darkened" understanding—because people are spiritually blind. They just can't see the truth of the Bible! This is why a brilliant scientist like Richard Dawkins can write of the death of Jesus in these terms:

> "I've described atonement, the central doctrine of Christianity, as vicious, sado-masochistic and repellent. We should also dismiss it as barking mad." (*The God Delusion*, page 253)

He just can't see that what he calls divine madness is really divine love! The scientifically brilliant man is a spiritually blind man.

Why is he blind? Paul is very blunt here—he says it is due to ignorance of God, to the wilful suppression of an awareness of God from creation (see Romans 1:18-21). Naturally, no one has any relational knowledge of God, because of the "hardening" of our hearts (Ephesians **4:18**)—an obstinate refusal in unbelievers to consider changing their minds. Behind intellectual objections lies a heart attitude. You may well have noticed that many people do set their own hearts in concrete, unable to recognise or appreciate spiritual truth and unwilling even to consider it. Sin is like a spiritual version of leprosy, that dreadful disease which renders people unfeeling in their limbs so that they constantly damage themselves. Sin is enslaving (an insatiable craving that people can't escape from), degenerative (it gets gradually worse so that sin that was once shocking is now indulged), and damaging (hurting not only those who are sinned against but also the sinners themselves).

Paul has exposed the progressive stages of sin: stubborn hardening of hearts leads to personal ignorance of God, which leads to darkened spiritual understanding... which in turn leads to evil behaviour, which he now describes.

A Trap, Not Liberty

If we can't remember from our personal experience before becoming a Christian, do we wonder how people spiral down into debauchery? Whether in the drunken excess of a nightclub on a Friday night or at a black-tie university society dinner, whether drooling over pole dancers in Soho, wife-swapping in the suburbs of Surrey or affairs among solicitors in a city firm—how does it all get so out of hand that marriages get destroyed and children get hurt? Because, having lost all the "sensitivity" to God with which we were created, people surrender themselves gradually to three kinds of wickedness (**v 19**): "sensuality" (meaning shameless debauchery), "impurity" (meaning riotous immorality) and "greed" (meaning insatiable appetites, because sin never truly satisfies). Although Paul is describing unbelievers, these appetites remain familiar to Christians (though thankfully fading gradually), because our sinful natures remain. Although God's Holy Spirit is slowly transforming us, we are still very much his work in progress.

What Paul is exposing is that immorality is not harmless fun, enlightened liberty, or an exciting tonic to spice up our marriages, as our media suggest. Immorality doesn't spice up marriages but, like acid, dissolves away trust; impurity is not harmless fun but, like a sewer, will foul up our friendships; and greed is not a good way to make progress for, like rust, it corrodes the inner soul of a man until he is utterly selfish. Why would we read magazines, watch programmes or admire friends who indulge in such fruitless deeds of darkness?

But who can help us when we are trapped in sensuality? When talking with one Christian man about the abject misery of himself and his new wife caused by his addiction to hard pornography, comparing sin to a prison cell proved helpful. Before we came to Christ, we were enslaved and captive to sin, hostages of Satan awaiting our death sentence under God's law. It's as if we were imprisoned in a stinking cell, and even though we sometimes gazed through the bars and wondered what life would be like outside, we couldn't leave. We lived in the darkness and dirt of the cell, unaware of how filthy we had become.

But on the cross, Christ paid the ransom price to open the door of our cell when he redeemed us with his precious blood (1:7). He has brought us out into the bright sunshine, blinking with amazement, as we began to realise in the light of the sun just how filthy we had become, and how beautiful life in the light can be. We now long to be clean like Jesus, but in our darker moments, perhaps after too much drink or in bad company or in self-pity, we crawl back into our old cell and curl up in the filth of "sensuality", "impurity" and "greed" (**4:19**). And because we're different now, we find it unbearably miserable. But the door of the cell is

> The blood of Christ has paid not only to set us free but to keep us free.

permanently open. The blood of Christ has paid not only to set us free but to keep us free to leave. And Jesus will repeatedly send people into our cell to pick us up and drag us out into the light once more—going sometimes willingly, sometimes reluctantly. And one day, when he returns to transform us for ever, he'll close the door behind us and we will never return to the filth again.

In the meantime, when we find ourselves wallowing in sin, it can be such a relief to admit to a trustworthy Christian friend or pastor that we need help. We need to be reminded of how good life in the light can be and that the door is opened for ever.

Recognising Ourselves

Do we recognise ourselves here? Are we living "as the Gentiles do" in some way (**v 17**)? Let us thank Jesus for paying the ransom to keep our cell door open even when we've crawled back into the filth. Let us confess our failures to him (Psalm 51 is David's great prayer for this) and seek his forgiveness, for John promises: "If we claim to be without sin, we deceive ourselves and the truth is not in us. If we confess our sins, he is faithful and just and will forgive us our sins and purify us from all unrighteousness" (1 John 1:8-9). And if we can't do it ourselves, let's ask a Christian friend to bring us out and keep us out. And when we're breathing the fresh air of life in the sunshine, we need to take any practical steps we can to barricade our path back into the cell, so we can't return to the darkness when we are feeling weak.

And let's be ready and available to rescue others in our churches from their cells with the gentle encouragements or firm rebukes they need. We must no longer live as the Gentiles do.

Questions for reflection

1. Why is it easier not to view "the Gentiles" as Paul does? How does a different view from Paul's affect our pursuit of holiness and our desire to evangelise?

2. When do you find it easiest to live as a chameleon? What would it look like to be Christ-like in that situation instead?

3. Is there anyone in your church who needs you to help them out of their "cell"? Will it require gentle encouragement or firm rebuke, do you think? How will you go about helping them?

PART TWO

Paul has told us how to stop blending in like chameleons. Now he turns to explaining how we can be distinctively holy in the heavenly realms. Again, it starts in our minds.

Renewed Thinking

In Ephesians **4:20-21**, Paul uses the language of school: "That, how-ever, is not the way of life you learned when you heard about Christ and were taught in him in accordance with the truth that is in Jesus." He speaks of having "learned" a new way of life and of being "taught ... the truth that is in Jesus" (**v 21**). This is the only time in Ephesians that Christ is called Jesus, because Paul is generally emphasising his en-thronement above all spiritual powers. But here, he reminds us that God has taught us by becoming a man, both to live a righteous Christian life for us and to practise what he preached to show us what he meant.

Holiness has been witnessed in the historical revelation of God in the person of Jesus as he is described in the pages of Scripture. The Bible is like a photograph of Jesus: if you enlarge a photograph enough, you will find that the picture is made of coloured dots—there are gaps be-tween the dots, but the picture is still accurate. So when you meet the person in the photograph, they are even more in real life what they are in the picture. In the same way, the words of the Bible are not every-thing there is to know about Jesus, but they do provide everything we need to know. The bits that are missing will be revealed when we meet him face to face, but they will be consistent with the Saviour we know from Scripture. This means that we truly get to know the real Jesus in the Bible and we hear the voice of his Spirit addressing us in the mean-ing of his text-message, in all its personal and spiritual power.

However, as Bible-loving people, we need to remember that we are saved by a person. Sometimes we speak of the saving knowledge of "the gospel", which stresses the heart of what we believe about him (that Jesus is Christ our Lord, who came as our King, died for our sins, rose to rule and will return to judge). Sometimes we speak of "the word" (the fuller explanation of the gospel in all of Scripture). Sometimes we speak of knowing "his grace" (that we're saved by God's ministry in Christ and not by our ministry in church). But we must also remember that we are saved by the person of whom all these things are true—Jesus—for being a Christian is not about trusting a formula, but about trusting a friend.

> Being a Christian is not about trusting a formula, but trusting a friend.

We're not saved merely by understanding some historic facts, but by the person of whom they are true. In the 1700s in Scotland, the followers of Robert Sandeman overreacted to the emotionalism of their day by proclaiming salvation through "bare belief in bare facts". This "Sandemanianism" was utterly dry and impersonally intellectual. Thankfully, a theologian called Andrew Fuller showed that biblical faith includes personal delight in the Jesus who is proclaimed in the gospel. We must avoid becoming Sandemanians, without personal delight in our Saviour. Saving faith is personal devotion to our Saviour. Being a Christian is learning to trust and delight in Christ!

Equally, we do not want to swing back to the other extreme and delight in a mythical Jesus who doesn't actually exist. Saving faith involves trusting with delight in the Lord and Saviour of whom the gospel of Scripture speaks, because of the historical things he has done. Sadly, the flagship Ephesian church would later be rebuked by the risen Jesus because, despite their impressive, sacrificial ministry and sound doctrine, they had forsaken their first love for Jesus. Their church has long disappeared (Revelation 2:1-7).

Learning How to Dress

Learning holiness from Jesus happens in three stages, which Paul likens to changing clothes. Our created personality remains throughout, but, like changing clothes, we take off our old grubby character in order to slowly get dressed again in the character of Christ. Like toddlers, we must learn to undress and dress ourselves properly.

So first, we must learn to undress ourselves. Being a Christian means being "taught, with regard to your former way of life, to put off your old self, which is being corrupted by its deceitful desires" (Ephesians **4:22**). We must learn consciously to put aside the lifestyle that is being "corrupted" by desires that are "deceitful"—deceitful because they promise satisfaction but in reality imprison us in misery now, and in hell later. Getting undressed prepares us to be "made new in the attitude of [our] minds" (**v 23**).

As we reject corrupted opinions, the Spirit of God will renew our attitudes within us through his word, so that new affections are created within us. We can't just aim to get rid of all desires—rather, our filthy desires must be replaced with clean desires. So we are not simply aiming to stop being envious and covetous for the partner or job or church we don't have; we need to learn to be grateful for the partner or job or church that God has given us!

Second, we must learn to dress ourselves properly: to "put on the new self, created to be like God in true righteousness and holiness" (**v 24**). To "put on the new self" is to acquire the character of Christ, who is righteous in his generous love, and holy in his disciplined purity.

This process begins with the gift of Christ's righteous holiness when we start trusting in Christ—we are permanently acceptable to God and seated in the heavenly realms (2:6) only through this "justification" (acceptance by God) by grace through faith in Christ (whose righteousness is reckoned to us so we are acceptable in him). Then we are taught to change and become in practice what we already are in status, through the ongoing work of sanctification by grace through faith, as we learn to trust and obey God's word.

I have attended some wonderful weddings over the years, including one recently in the ballroom of the prestigious Savoy Hotel in central London. Imagine if I needed to borrow a "morning suit" because

I didn't have one of my own and I couldn't afford to hire or buy one. So I borrow a very expensive morning suit from a generous friend. Imagine if my friend said I could keep his suit and wear it as my own in future. That is like what God has done. He has "imputed" to us (counted as ours) the righteousness of his Son. He has clothed us in Christ's perfect righteousness, which qualifies us to enter the kingdom of heaven, just as I am able to enter the Savoy Hotel in my borrowed morning suit. And it was incredibly expensive for God to do this—he had to swap places with us, and sacrificed himself in Christ on a cross to suffer our hell, so we can have access to his wedding banquet, clothed in his holy life.

Now, having acquired such an expensive morning suit, I wouldn't want to just wear the new trousers over my filthy jeans or the new waistcoat over my sweaty T-shirt! To do so would diminish the value of what I was given. I would want to take off my dirty clothes. Likewise, when we become a Christian, God accepts us permanently in Christ's righteousness. But he doesn't want us to carry on sinning—as if nothing much has happened. It diminishes the seriousness of our sin and the cost of what Christ has provided for us! We are saved completely by his holiness—but we are saved for a new life of learning holiness! Now that we are permanently clothed in the holy character of Christ, we should learn to take off our old sinfulness and wear the holy character of Christ. Such holiness demonstrates to the spiritual powers in the spiritual realms the wisdom of his reconciliation under Christ through his death.

Christian Clothing

What does this look like in practice? Paul now explains this with some practical examples. They are all areas where our behaviour will either destroy the unity of a church and its witness in the heavenly realms, or strengthen it:

1. *No more falsehood* (**4:25**): "Therefore each of you must put off falsehood and speak truthfully to your neighbour, for we are all members of one body." Paul is here picking up the Old Testament

promise of Zechariah 8 that God's new people in the "Faithful City" will speak the truth to their neighbours. We must be honest with each other, like people belonging to one body of Christ. This requires speaking truthfully about each other (no more gossiping or damning with faint praise), speaking truthfully to each other (no more exaggeration and lying), and being conscious of the truth of the gospel of grace (no more hypocritical criticism).

2. *No more anger* (**v 26-27**): "'In your anger do not sin': Do not let the sun go down while you are still angry, and do not give the devil a foothold." Paul recognises that it is sometimes appropriate to be angry—for instance, when brothers and sisters in Christ around the world are being persecuted or if someone has been hurt by someone else in our church. But we're not to indulge our anger so that it becomes self-important righteous indignation. Paul says it's wise to adopt a time limit for grievances—to give up our causes and campaigns by the end of any day, so that Satan can't gain an opportunity to build up divisive factions that destroy the church over time.

3. *No more stealing* (**v 28**): "Anyone who has been stealing must steal no longer, but must work, doing something useful with their own hands, that they may have something to share with those in need." Paul recognises that in the godless lifestyle we once lived in, we may have been stealing: whether permanently "borrowing" tools from work that we never return, or overcharging clients, or falsely claiming expenses or avoiding taxes. Christians have to stop sharp practices and work hard, not to spend excessively on ourselves, but to contribute to the needs of others in our family and church, and beyond that to gospel work, especially among the poor. We are no longer to use our hands to get, but to give.

4. *No more unwholesome talk* (**v 29**): "Do not let any unwholesome talk come out of your mouths, but only what is helpful for building others up according to their needs, that it may benefit those

who listen." The word "unwholesome" is literally "rotten"—it refers to vulgar jokes, damaging gossip or spiteful criticism, which need to be replaced with wholesome language and words that encourage and strengthen the faith of others.

5. *No more grieving the Holy Spirit* (**v 30**): "Do not grieve the Holy Spirit of God, with whom you were sealed for the day of redemption." Paul refers here to the rebellions of Israel, on their way to the promised land, which so grieved the Spirit of God (Isaiah 63:10). He calls upon his readers, who have been sealed as belonging to God with his Spirit, not to grieve him by repeatedly rebelling against God with endless, discontented grumbling and moral disobedience, which will not testify to the grace of God in the spiritual realms.

6. *No more malice* (**v 31**): "Get rid of all bitterness, rage and anger, brawling and slander, along with every form of malice." We are now able, in the power of the Spirit of Christ, to repent of resentful and envious bitterness towards siblings who have what we want or friends who have hurt us in the past; we can pray for strength not to react to those who annoy us with a raging temper or seething anger; we can resolve to avoid drunken brawling, and instead of slandering others can resolve only to speak well of them. Indeed, we can gradually replace all our malicious instincts towards those who malign us with a little of the grace that Christ showed towards his enemies, including us.

But what motivation is there for getting changed so dramatically? Paul gives two.

First, we are to "be kind and compassionate to one another, forgiving each other, just as in Christ God forgave [us]" (**v 32**). We can learn to be generously kind, gently compassionate and mutually forgiving, from the way that God has graciously forgiven us. So when someone repents, however weakly, we can resolve never to bring their sin up again before them, never to bring it up again before other people, never to bring it up again before our own minds, and never to bring it up again before God in our prayers, because God forgave us when our repentance was so very shallow. And until they repent, we can give our desires for revenge over to God, who ensures that justice is done, and ask him for the willingness to show mercy and seek reconciliation, however weakly their repentance is eventually offered, because the God who should punish us in hell for ever has forgiven us. I recall a missionary called James being publicly asked if he could forgive the violent men who shot and disfigured him in the face and raped his wife in front of him. James replied: "I can forgive them because my Father in heaven has forgiven me for so much more".

And second, we are to "follow God's example ... live a life of love" (5:1-2)—we are not to be chameleons imitating the world, but Christians imitating God, especially in the sacrificial love of his death. At Calvary, Christ "gave himself up for us as a fragrant offering and sacrifice to God" (v 2). To follow God's example is to love, not just with a cold, antiseptic absence of immorality, but with a love that is willing to make sacrifices for the salvation and blessing of others. For this is "fragrant" to God (v 2)—it pleases him, and testifies to the wisdom of his plans in the spiritual realms.

> Christian love is not a cold, antiseptic absence of immorality, but a willingness to make sacrifices for others.

So when we gaze into this passage like a mirror, how are we dressed? Are we clothed in the fashions of the world, wearing the dirty garments of darkened understanding that leads to sensuality, like chameleons trying to stay camouflaged and avoid predators? Or are we being renewed in our minds by God through his word, putting on the holiness of Christ in kindness and compassion and sacrificial love?

What do you need to take off? And what do you need to put on? Ask God to help you get changed, so that you no longer live like a chameleon, conformed to the culture around you, but as a Christian, conformed to the Christ who died in his love for us.

Questions for reflection

1. How can you make sure you continue to delight in a relationship with the real Jesus, and avoid dry intellectualism?

2. How have you experienced the Spirit helping you to take off your "old self" and wear your "new self"? How has doing so changed your life for the better?

3. Look over the old-self vs new-self differences described on pages 141-142. Which encourage you as you look at your own life; which challenge you; and which are new for you?

9. LIVE IN THE LIGHT

It's vital to learn from the debates of church history, for as the philosopher George Santayana famously said:

"Those who cannot remember the past are condemned to repeat it."

We will only avoid the mistakes of church history if we learn from the great scholars who contended with the massive theological challenges of the past that threatened to derail Christ's churches in every generation. For example, the divinity of Christ, clarified by **Athanasius** against **Arius**, is vital for our debate with Muslims; the seriousness of sin, established by **Augustine** against **Pelagius**, is critical for our debate with liberals, who deny the reality of hell; the justification of believers by faith alone, championed by **Luther** against Rome, is vital for our debates with Roman Catholicism; and the sovereignty of God in salvation, articulated by Calvin against the "**Arminians**" of his day, remains vital for avoiding the deceptions of self-styled "open theists", who deny that God is in control of the future.

But in our era, we face new challenges. The debate that is currently tearing Western Christianity apart is the necessity of holiness for salvation. In general, liberal church leaderships have compromised biblical standards of sexual immorality—of which homosexual activity is the most controversial example. For since Western secular culture is firmly in favour of sexual expression without biblical restraint, churches that follow the culture will be more popular and have an easier life. To lower our standards of sexual purity—or at least to keep quiet about them—is going to become increasingly attractive, as we see unbelievers and government authorities increasingly hostile to our message and to us because of our restrictive sexual **ethics**, and as we bear an increasingly high cost for publicly standing against the tide of society and of institutional churches that compromise. Thankfully, we can turn to a great Christian scholar who battled with the extreme sexual **hedonism** of his day and clarified some simple timeless principles that spell out the will of God for us today: the apostle Paul.

We've been learning from this epistle that God's glorious eternal plan is to unite all things under Christ (chapter 1), through the death and resurrection of Christ (chapter 2), which is demonstrated in the spiritual dimension by his church (chapter 3). But the wisdom of God is only displayed where the members of his heavenly church actually do repent from immorality to live under the rule of Christ in his holiness. This passage tells us with uncompromising clarity that repentance from immorality and pursuit of Christ-like holiness have always been necessary for salvation.

Imitating God

In chapters 4 – 6, Paul is applying the great gospel truths of chapters 1 – 3 to the life of the local church. He began this second half of the letter in 4:1 by urging his readers to "live [literally "walk"] a life worthy of the calling you have received". This call to "live ... worthy" is then repeated in 4:17 and again, to introduce both halves of our passage, in **5:2** ("live a life of love") and **5:8** ("live as children of light"). Paul urgently wants his readers to consider the appropriate way for Christians to live distinctively in response to their reconciliation to God and to each other under Christ.

The previous passage drew a stark contrast between how we live before and after we've been saved. In this passage, Paul draws an even more dramatic contrast between behaviour outside and inside the church.

This contrast begins with Paul's conclusion from chapter 4: "Follow God's example, therefore, as dearly loved children and live a life of love, just as Christ loved us and gave himself up for us as a fragrant offering and sacrifice to God" (**5:1-2**). The fundamentally distinctive characteristic of the Christian lifestyle should be that we now live "just as Christ loved us". We are to be Christ-shaped rather than culture-shaped. So we must "live a life of love"—a life lived for the good of others. As he "gave himself" for us, we must give ourselves to others in voluntary self-sacrifice. Since Christ died "for us as a fragrant offering and sacrifice to God"—for the salvation of sinners, and pleasing to God—so we must make sacrifices for the salvation of others to please God. Distinctive Christian living is self-sacrificial love… for the salvation of others… to please God. Notice that our ethic is not just the absence of wickedness but the presence of love; not just the rejection of impurity but the practice of grace towards others. Bible-believing Christians often have a reputation for what we deny and reject, but not a matching reputation for gracious generosity towards others. Let us pray for strength to become like Jesus—who was not only without sin but full of kindness—even towards those that hate us.

But in chapter 5, Paul begins with the negative…

Three "No's"

Paul clarifies God's high standards of sexual holiness: "But among you there must not be even a hint of sexual immorality, or of any kind of impurity, or of greed" (**v 3**). Here he says "no" to three vices: sexual immorality, impurity, and greed.

"Sexual immorality" translates the Greek word *pornei* (from which we get words like pornography), which means any sexual activity outside marriage (even if it's between consenting adults). If people accuse us of being homophobic, we need to explain that we are not homophobic but "pornophobic", which is much wider. Such sexual activity includes watching pornography or reading erotic novels, visiting strip shows or brothels, flirting or lusting, and extra-marital masturbation. As difficult as we may find this in our sexually overheated society, this also rules out all sexual activity before and outside marriage. God is not against sex—he invented it as the thrilling and intimate glue for the life-long union of one man and one woman in marriage! God is simply against abusing his beautiful gift, because sex is intended as the intense display of his wisdom in bringing people under the blessing of Christ's rule. When sex is misused, our Creator knows that people will soon get hurt

"Impurity" is a broader vice that includes sexual lust, but also includes other sorts of licentiousness—whether drunkenness, lewd conversations or riotous behaviour. This word is not condemning godly joking, fun, dancing or partying. It is about crudeness—and most of us can recognise the difference by asking ourselves whether Jesus would be happy with it.

"Greed" is an unrestrained desire for more money, food, property or other material things. It makes us covetous of what others do have and bitter about what we don't. It is the great unconfessed sin of the Western middle classes. We're not to be **ascetics**, denying the goodness of God's gifts of material prosperity—Paul warns Timothy that Satan inflames pointless self-denial to make God seem mean; and encourages us to enjoy God's gifts, like food and marriage, in accordance with his word, with thankfulness (1 Timothy 4:1-4). But for most of us, that is not our main problem. What we struggle with is the temptation to be hedonistic, indulging our appetites for pleasure and comfort and hoarding material wealth; instead of being joyful givers like God, and modest in our lifestyle (eg: "Give me neither poverty nor riches, but give me only my daily bread", Proverbs 30:8), in order to be sacrificially generous to others, especially for the work of the gospel. This will feel painful; but if our generosity isn't hurting, then it isn't actually sacrificial.

> If our generosity isn't hurting, then it isn't actually sacrificial.

There cannot "be even a hint" of these ungodly things in our lifestyle or conversation, because they're so serious to God—"these are improper for God's holy people" (Ephesians **5:3**). If we want to be in God's family, we have to be different now. God's family is not just any old family with low standards, but the family of the holy, almighty God—we have to step up! This includes our words as much as our deeds: Paul insists that: "obscenity, foolish talk or coarse joking ... are out of place" (**v 4**). If immoral activity is inappropriate, then filthy language that makes light of such sin is also improper. It's quite possible to be entertaining and hilarious without being dirty or vulgar, as Christian comedians like Milton Jones, Tim Hawkins and Tim Vine wonderfully demonstrate!

The antidote to us indulging our self-serving lust for sexual immorality, licentious impurity or acquisitive greed is to recognise the true worth of what our loving heavenly Father has already given us, rather than lusting for what he hasn't. It's important for churches to clarify for believers and unbelievers alike that Christians delight in God's gift of sex within marriage. But we don't think that sex defines us, so those who are sexually inactive can still be completely satisfied in Christ. Paul clarifies the healthy alternative to hedonism as "thanksgiving" (**v 4**). We can be giving thanks to God for his overflowing generosity, especially in our extravagant spiritual blessings in Christ (1:1-14), whether or not we are having sex, or good sex, or enough sex. The fundamental solution to immorality, impurity and greed is nothing more complicated than thanksgiving, because sexual disobedience in Christians is generally caused to some degree by the spiritual amnesia of forgetting God's grace and then feeling sorry for ourselves and entitled to indulge our sinful appetites.

The Bible's Sexual Ethics

It's helpful for us to pause here to briefly survey the Bible's background to this text on sexual ethics.

Fundamentally, we are made in the image of God. This is the foundation of Christian thinking on humanity (and relationships within humanity). Jesus endorsed the teaching of Scripture, that there is only one God, who is a unity of three Persons, Father, Son and Holy Spirit. And this God designed mankind to be like him, for relationship with him: "God created mankind in his own image, in the image of God he created them; male and female he created them" (Genesis 1:27).

Since we are made like him, human beings flourish in relationships that are shaped like God. This has profound effects upon all our human relationships:

- *God is permanent in eternity:* so humans prosper in lasting rather than transitory relationships. This is why it's so damaging for children to be moved around foster homes, and why we all generally tend to flourish in lasting marriages, friendships and communities.

- *God is plural:* so humans flourish in families and communities more than in lonely isolation (including a virtual world on screen). This is why humans flourish in the plurality and love required of marriage, and why family life is to be treasured and protected.

- *God is equal:* so human beings of every age, race, economic status and sexuality are equally precious to God. This is why godly Christians invest so sacrificially in social welfare, and why we must care enough about those caught in unrepentant sexual immorality not to lie to them.

- *God is complementary:* so human beings flourish better in harmonious diverse social contexts than in **homogeneous** social environments. This is why God made humanity male and female, and why marriage is intended by God to be heterosexual (the clues are anatomical).

- *God is ordered:* so in all our relationships we flourish with roles of loving authority and submission that don't imply any superiority or inferiority. As Christ leads the church but submits to the Father, someone can be in authority over her children and staff team and submit to the authority of her employer and husband, and yet still be absolutely equal in importance and dignity with them all.

- *God is loving:* so the most important aspect in all our relationships is to be loving. This is not merely sentimental affection or sensual desire or feelings of compatibility, nor based upon the performance or appearance of another. Love is a commitment to serve the interests of another. So Christians understand marriage as the union of a man and a woman established by mutual public promises to love each other, as church marriage services sometimes quaintly put it, "for better, for worse; for richer, for poorer; in sickness and in health". Paul will say much more about this in the next passage—for the marriage relationship is placed at the heart of human society as a powerful illustration of the love of Christ for his church, and of God's wisdom in gathering all things under Christ in the heavenly realms.

As Christ's sacrificial love for his church is a permanent and complementary spiritual union, so our marriages are intended to be permanent (not broken by divorce) and complementary (heterosexual and not homosexual) physical unions (expressed sexually and not only in friendships).

The most prominent clash between Western cultural thinking and God's word currently is the Bible's condemnation of homosexual practice, and its teaching about marriage. You may hear prominent church leaders suggesting that the Christian gospel is primarily about in inclusion, so that committed and faithful homosexual relationships should be welcomed and blessed in church. You will always be able to find a scholar trying to reconstruct a possible first-century culture that will allow us to interpret texts in the way we want to, in order to be popular in the world today. But the fact is that God uses strong language in calling homosexual practice "shameful", "unnatural" and "perversion" (Romans 1:26, Jude 7). He warns in 1 Corinthians 6:9-10: "Do not be deceived: neither the sexually immoral nor idolaters nor adulterers nor men who have sex with men nor thieves nor the greedy nor drunkards nor slanderers nor swindlers will inherit the kingdom of God". Notice that active homosexuality is listed as a behaviour that, if not repented of, leaves someone outside God's kingdom eternally—but also that it does this no more nor less than other sins, such as greed or drunkenness or slander.

The challenge is plain: we simply must love those of us who struggle with same-sex attraction enough not to lie about their salvation. The gospel is not a message of God's inclusion without change, but of God's salvation with power to change. Sam Allberry, a British pastor and author who has for many years experienced same-sex attraction, puts it wisely and helpfully:

> "The Bible is very clear that God loves everyone, and welcomes us into his family, the church, through faith in Christ, whatever our gender, class or race and, we might say, sexuality. We do need to keep stressing that. But we also need to recognise the fact that the Bible is consistently negative about homosexual sex and, indeed, any sex outside of heterosexual marriage."
>
> (Interview in *Evangelicals Now*, October 2012)

Our fundamental identity and value lie in being created in the image of God rather than in our gender or sexuality. Positively, this is why Christians can celebrate being a child, or single, or widowed, just as much as being someone who is sexually active. All are equal in worth; all can be equally fulfilled in life. But equally, since we are those made in the image of God, who is Christ, and are designed to reflect that image, we must listen to, and teach, what God says about how to live in his image—and that requires us to affirm that sex outside heterosexual marriage is sinful, however unpopular that may be for a season.

For, as Paul says, echoing his words to the Corinthian church, which we have already seen: "Of this you can be sure: no immoral, impure or greedy person—such a person is an idolater—has any inheritance in the kingdom of Christ and of God" (Ephesians **5:5**). There are countless issues about which no one can be certain, but of this you can be absolutely certain: those who habitually live in unrepentant sexual immorality, licentious impurity or material greed (not in occasional repented sins but as a settled lifestyle) are idolaters, because they are devoted to their desires instead of God. If unrepentant, such people cannot have any inheritance from God in his kingdom.

There has always been, and will always be, someone ready to offer an easier and a more acceptable ethic than the Bible's; so Paul counsels us to "let no one deceive you with empty words, for because of such things God's wrath comes on those who are disobedient" (**v 6**). Many—even within the church—are trying to deceive us. But we must not be deceived, and must not become "partners with them" (**v 7**), so that we can call a dying world to life, a dark world to light, and a world under judgment to be living under the grace of Christ.

> There has always been, and will always be, someone ready to offer an easier ethic than the Bible's.

If we become like the world, we will no longer be a demonstration of God's wisdom in the heavenly realms. It is when we submit to the rule of Christ that God is glorified in his church.

Questions for reflection

1. Does the command to live with "not even a hint" of sexual immorality challenge you in any way? Do you need to ask God for forgiveness and commit to changing, with his help?

2. How can you, and your church, ensure you are talking about sex with thanksgiving, rather than being silent or only negative about it?

3. Why is it important in Western societies to remember that "our fundamental identity and value lie in being created in the image of God rather than in our gender or sexuality"? How might this help you to speak to others about why biblical sexual ethics are good news, not oppressive news?

PART TWO

Children of Light

Moving from the negative to the positive, from what we avoid to what we nurture, Paul urges his readers then and now to "live as children of light" (**v 8**).

"For you were once darkness, but now you are light in the Lord." This means we must be motivated not only by the severe consequences of sin, but by the profound change that God has accomplished within us. It's not just that we live in the light of the gospel of Christ, but we *are* "light in the Lord". It's not just that we have new surroundings, but that we are reborn in the new humanity of Christ (2:11-22), with his spiritual character of light, as children of the God who is light. Paul says in **5:9** that the natural product or "fruit" of this character is the loving generosity of Christ's goodness, the willing obedience of Christ's righteousness and a delight in the honesty of Christ's truth. A true desire to live in this way will mean a commitment to discovering "what pleases the Lord" (**v 10**)—the fundamental daily practice of discovering from his word how we can please our new Lord, rather than indulging ourselves or desperately pleasing others.

This will inevitably mean rejecting worldly ways: "Have nothing to do with the fruitless deeds of darkness, but rather expose them" (**v 11**). The deeds of darkness don't produce any useful fruit. So we are not to ignore or hide them in ourselves or our church; or, like mice under the floorboards, they will multiply unless we expose them to get rid of them. Notice that these verses follow **verse 7**, where Paul tells us to take care about who we choose to be "partners" with; especially, of course, in who we marry—they "must belong to the Lord" (1 Corinthians 7:39).

One aspect of Christian maturity is to be intentional about what influences we accept. Sharing our lives with other Christians will helpfully expose the areas where we are living in the dark and help us to learn how to live in the light (Ephesians **5:11**). So try to share life with more mature Christians in a Bible-believing church, rather than being an irreg-ular consumer. Don't just listen to sermons but join in with the prayer meeting and small groups. For if you take a hot coal away from the fire, it quickly goes cold. Put the coal back on the fire and it becomes red hot again! Some believers never really thrive in holiness because they remain aloof and disengaged from other believers. But if we invest time and energy in making friends with Christians, we will begin to catch the lifestyle of light and replace the habits of darkness.

So what will it mean to "have nothing to do with the fruitless deeds of darkness" (**v 11**)? In one sense, the key word here is "nothing". The story is told of a billionaire with a luxury yacht who was inter-viewing potential helmsmen to skipper it. As the best three applicants gathered on the boat to demonstrate their sailing skills to him, he explained that he wanted a sailor of great skill who would be available to take him and his friends or clients sailing whenever he needed. The successful applicant would, of course, be handsomely rewarded. Each of the three men took turns to showcase their skills out in the harbour. The first sailed the priceless yacht at top speed within 30 metres of the rocky cliffs. Everyone gasped at his talent. The second helmsman was even more skilful. He sailed the yacht within 15 metres of the cliffs. All were breathless with excitement and also some trepidation about what the third would attempt. The third candidate calmly steered the yacht out into the middle of the harbour and all enjoyed a rather relax-ing trip around the harbour, admiring the stunning views.

To their great surprise, the billionaire gave the job to the third applicant. "You were all amazingly skilful," he said. "But my yacht is precious and I don't want a helmsman who is so confident as to be tempted to steer it within a few metres of crashing on the rocks. One mistake and it's a disaster. I want a man who will take my pre-cious yacht out into the open water to enjoy the safety and beauty that's there!"

God does not want us to be driving our precious bodies as close to immorality as we can. We may get away with it for a while, but one mistake and we live with the wreckage for the rest of our lives on earth. Actually there is great joy and satisfaction in living well within God's rules. So why are you seeing that colleague after work for a drink when you know he'll flirt with you and you fancy him? Why have you agreed to go clubbing with colleagues while you're abroad on business when you know you'll feel pressured to drink and go to a strip joint? Why haven't you asked your partner to block the "Adult" cable channels on your TV, and your Bible-study leader to sort out an internet accountability program? Why are you sharing your personal thoughts with someone else's husband, and why are you stopping to chat when you drop off that married youth leader after church? Stop steering close to the rocks: have nothing to do with the fruitless deeds of darkness.

After all, "it is shameful even to mention what the disobedient do in secret" (**v 12**). Paul doesn't mean we can't talk honestly, but he does mean we want to avoid a culture of talking about sin that normalises and dignifies and excuses it. This involves talking about wholesome and encouraging things over a drink or a meal, instead of simply swapping the godless gossip of the world. We need to move on from trying desperately to belong in the world to enjoying belonging to Jesus.

> We want to avoid a culture of normalising, dignifying and excusing sin.

Christ has come as the light of the world so "everything exposed by the light" of Christ in his word "becomes visible, for it is light that makes everything visible" (**v 13-14**, NIV84). Paul then quotes from Isaiah, explaining that "this is why it is said: 'Wake up, sleeper, rise from the dead, and Christ will shine on you'" (**v 14**). He is referring to the glorious promise of Isaiah 60:1: "Arise, shine, for your light has come, and the glory of the LORD rises upon you". Since Christ has risen from the grave to reveal himself as the light of the world from God, we must now wake up and live by his teaching. The lamp of the gospel has been switched on in our old prison cell of sin to reveal the true squalor of the world.

Be Careful, Be Filled

And so we are to "be very careful, then, how [we] live" (Ephesians **5:15**). We must be "wise", considering carefully how we are actually living. We should make "the most of every opportunity" (**v 16**) because the days are evil. This means taking every chance to serve Christ in the light, whether speaking about Christ to a colleague at work, or helping teach Scripture in the children's classes at church, or inviting an elderly neighbour to church. We are to see every day as an opportunity to proclaim Christ, in order to gather people under Christ before he returns in terrifying judgment.

Paul warns his readers to be careful: to live "not as unwise but as wise, making the most of every opportunity, because the days are evil. Therefore do not be foolish, but understand what the Lord's will is" (**v 15-17**).

And part of the Lord's will for our lives is that we "do not get drunk on wine" (**v 18**). Don't be filled with booze. Although in moderation it gladdens the heart (and Song of Songs recognises that it lowers our inhibitions for intimacy in a marriage), too much wine and beer often leads to "debauchery". Many Western Christians are quietly failing to contain their drinking levels, and Proverbs describes the sad lifestyle that brings:

"Who has woe? Who has sorrow? Who has strife? Who has complaints? Who has needless bruises? Who has bloodshot eyes? Those who linger over wine, who go to sample bowls of mixed wine. Do not gaze at wine when it is red, when it sparkles in the cup, when it goes down smoothly! In the end it bites like a snake and poisons like a viper. Your eyes will see strange sights and your mind will imagine confusing things. You will be like one sleeping on the high seas, lying on top of the rigging. 'They hit me,' you will say, 'but I'm not hurt! They beat me, but I don't feel it! When will I wake up so I can find another drink?'"

(Proverbs 23:29-35)

Does this sound familiar? Enjoy God's gifts, but don't get drunk!

Instead, says Paul, "be filled" with God's Holy Spirit (Ephesians **5:18**)—which, the parallel passage in Colossians 3:16 explains, happens as we let the Spirit's message of Christ dwell richly in every part of our lives. We are to be people who are "under the influence" of the Holy Spirit, and not alcohol. This will issue, not in debauchery, but in all kinds of joyful "psalms, hymns, and songs from the Spirit" (Ephesians **5:19**) that build each other up.

So Paul tells us to sing and make music in our hearts to the Lord, privately and publicly, because we are designed as emotional beings to feel the glory of the gospel in our guts, that we may give God the praise that he is due, and also to practise our evangelism (when we praise God to others). Some of us may have been raised in an unhealthily anti-emotional culture and need to pray that God will open our lips that we may declare his praises (see Psalm 51:15). Others of us have been raised in an overemotional and sentimental culture, and we will need to ensure that we are singing the truths of the word of God, and not just vacuous "Jesus is my girlfriend"-style songs! But singing is not optional; singing is commanded by Paul because the nature of God expressed in the gospel is grace in salvation, to which it is necessary to respond in grateful faith with our whole being.

Indeed, in contrast to the ingratitude of sin (Romans 1:21), the core of Christian faith in the gospel of grace is thankfulness as we enjoy our freedom from sin. So let's be "always giving thanks to God the Father for everything, in the name of our Lord Jesus Christ" (Ephesians **5:20**). Sin is essentially rebellious and complaining ungratefulness; and holiness is essentially a life of gratitude for all that God has graciously given us in Christ. This is the triumphant wisdom displayed in the heavenly realms by the church of God. The heart of living in the light of the gospel is to live with grateful joy to God for Jesus Christ.

Questions for reflection

1. Is there any way in which you are compromising with "the fruit-less deeds of darkness", rather than having nothing to do with them? Do you need to make practical changes in some way?

2. How can you pursue being most influenced by the Spirit, rather than by alcohol or something else?

3. How will you make sure your singing in church next Sunday is an overflow of your love for the Lord Jesus?

10. A MARRIAGE MADE IN HEAVEN

In most Western cultures, with divorce rates rising, marriages rates falling and more couples co-habiting and having children without marrying, even the most romantic and glamorous royal wedding can't obscure the obvious question: is marriage really necessary anymore? And with the legal redefinition of marriage allowing for same-sex marriages in many nations now, how should Christians conduct their marriages?

In this passage we'll find that marriage has been instilled within the instincts of humanity and into the fabric of human society by our loving Creator to stir up human longing and prepare our hearts for the love of Christ. Marriage conducted by Christians in God's way is a glorious demonstration in the heavenly realms of the triumph of his plan to gather all things under Christ. Among God's people, marriage is no longer a battleground, but a field of victory, where sinners can remain united to each other in the service of Christ! Indeed, it is given by God as the most powerful illustration of Christ's covenant love for his church. So for all of us, whether single, married, divorced, widowed or in any condition of marriage, this beautiful passage not only speaks of the things we can pray for those who are married, but celebrates the intimate spiritual union of all believers with Christ, to whom we will one day be united—the ultimate "marriage made in heaven". This is not a section just for married people, for Paul says in **verse 32**: "I am talking about Christ and the church"!

Submit to One Another

The apostle concludes his previous description of the behaviour of Spirit-filled people and opens this new section with a general principle that summarises his teaching about behaviour in Christian households: "Submit to one another out of reverence for Christ" (**v 21**). In all forty occurrences in the New Testament, the word "submit" means to arrange yourself under someone's authority, as soldiers accept the authority of their commanding officers.

Some have suggested this means that Christians should all submit to each other (which sounds fair, but is actually impossible). Some have suggested that Paul means that Christians should live lives that are generally submissive to authorities of all kinds. The best view is that he's introducing this new topic of submission in various household relationships; namely, of wives to their husbands, children to their parents, and slaves to their masters. The motivation is to be "reverence" (literally fear) of Christ, our holy Lord and powerful Judge. In each of these relationships, the person who is called to submit is addressed first, and then the person in authority—each time with an instruction followed by a motivation in Christ. Everyone will be accountable to him, and those he has redeemed will long to please him…

This household code, like its parallels in Colossians 3:18-25 and 1 Peter 2:18 – 3:7, would probably have seemed reassuringly conservative for the Greco-Roman culture of the time, in preserving order in the household. As in most cultures around the world in every age, the family unit was regarded as the bedrock of human flourishing. But distinctively and radically for the time, the biblical principle of the equality and dignity of all persons is forcibly emphasised here. Each person is addressed as responsible before God for their own behaviour. In each relationship someone is required to exercise authority to lead and the other is required to submit gladly to that leadership. But neither is more important or less important than the other.

Who God is Shapes What Marriage is

Paul's teaching here reflects the profoundly Christian understanding of humanity being dignified by our creation in the image of God. Indeed, contrary to much contemporary thinking, our fundamental identity and value are in being created by and for God, rather than in being married or sexually active. That's why Christians celebrate the dignity of childhood, celibate singleness and widowhood, as well as the intimacy of marriage (and that's why Christians should not be pressuring believers to marry, when Paul celebrates the benefits of singleness for someone's gospel ministry in 1 Corinthians 7). And this explains why God designed marriage as the lifelong union of one man and one woman, not primarily for our mutual happiness, but primarily for our partnership in serving God. This again means that saved sinners, gathered together under the rule of Christ in a marriage, powerfully proclaim the triumphant wisdom of the eternal plan of God. We discover that we are more blessed as we serve him together than if we make our own happiness our governing idol. As two cyclists focused on the road ahead can enjoy travelling very closely but will crash if they are constantly gazing intently at each other, so a husband and wife who make serving the gospel of Christ their shared goal can enjoy being much closer together than if they are focused entirely upon their own happiness.

> Our fundamental identity and value are in being created by and for God, rather than in being married or sexually active.

This is especially evident in raising children to fill the earth with the knowledge of God (as Genesis 1 says we are created to do), in order to gather more people under Christ.

As discussed in an earlier chapter, it's best to consider the nature of God before trying to understand his rules for our behaviour in marriage. Jesus endorsed the teaching of Scripture, that there is only one God, who is a unity of three Persons—Father, Son and Holy Spirit. This profoundly affects Christian marriage.

The holy Trinity of God lives in a permanent, plural, equal, complementary, ordered, loving union. Since we're created like him, we thrive in marriage relationships like his trinitarian union. Since God is permanent, God designed us for lasting marriages rather than divorce. Since God is plural, God designed us for marriages of intimate companionship expressed sexually to counteract loneliness. Since God is three equal Persons, God designed us for marriages in which husbands and wives are equally dignified. Since God is diverse and complementary, God has created the relationship of marriage to be diverse and wonderfully complementary, in a heterosexual rather than homosexual union (the clues are anatomical, whatever a government legislates; and any other relationship cannot be marriage before God). Since God's Trinity is ordered, with God the Son and God the Holy Spirit gladly submitting to God the Father, so he has designed all human relationships, including marriage, with authority exercised lovingly and submission given willingly without any implication of superiority or inferiority.

It is crucial to understand that, in biblical thinking, order does not imply inequality because God is an ordered Trinity. So, as Christ rules over the church but also submits to his Father (yet is equal with him), we may have different roles in different relationships: someone may exercise loving authority over her children and her colleagues; willingly submit to the authority of her employer, her church elders and her husband; yet be absolutely equal in importance and dignity with them all.

Supremely, since God is loving within his own Trinity, so he has designed us for loving marriages. As he has committed himself sacrificially to us in covenanted and exclusive love, so the most precious aspect of all our human relationships, and especially marriage, is to love and be loved, not merely with sentimental affection or sensual desire, but with sustained sacrificial kindness in every season of life—

an unconditional love based not upon the other's glamorous looks, but upon a commitment to be exclusively devoted to their best interests. And what a stunningly wonderful blessing a happy Christian marriage is!

Having understood how the nature of God impacts the marriage relationship, we're better placed to understand his commands for our behaviour within marriage.

But why does Paul begin with marriage? Guessing at contexts is a risky business that often leads to twisted interpretation. What is plain from this letter, dedicated to explaining God's plan to unite all things together under Christ in the church, is that the union of husband and wife in marriage is a fundamental part of that united church community. If a church is to be united, it will need united marriages! It's therefore no coincidence that the first household relationship Paul addresses specifically is marriage.

As we will see, since the husband is the "head" of his wife (Ephesians **5:23**), the health of a marriage will depend primarily on the husband getting his act together. But Paul begins with the role of wives—and his teaching is simple and brief.

A Word to Wives

Wives are directly instructed to "submit yourselves to your own husbands" (**v 22**), not in an enforced, servile oppression (as in some religious cultures, and too often in the history of the church), but voluntarily: it is not for her husband to make her submit. She is to submit "as to the Lord" (NIV84)—as part of her service of Christ, and in accordance with God's great plan to bring everything together under Christ (even though it is often sneered at today). This is a role—a temporary role in this world—required by her Lord.

The reason is that, whether we like it or not, "the husband is the head of the wife as Christ is the head of the church" (**v 23**). In 1:22 Christ is described as the head who governs the cosmos, and in 4:15

as the head who lovingly rules and cares for his church. However politically incorrect this may sound, we must recognise that God requires husbands to exercise loving rule and care as the head, or leader, of their wives, who are required to accept it. At creation, God made a wife for Adam from him (she is like him), after him (he leads her) and for him (because he was lonely without her) (Genesis 2:18-24). Paul simply reminds the Ephesians in the most general terms that the church is Christ's body, and that he "gave himself up for her" (Ephesians **5:25**)—and that the relationship between wife and husband mirrors this. That doesn't mean that a wife is her husband's body. A husband and wife are united in one body but this doesn't mean that their separate identities are erased to make them the same. Nor does it mean that he is her eternal saviour. It does mean that, wherever possible, he will love her enough to want to rescue her from trouble of every kind.

And so, Paul says in **verse 24**, the submission of the church to Christ in everything is to be the model for a wife submitting to her husband. As the church submits to Christ in confident expectation of receiving his loving care, accepting that his rule is for her benefit, appreciating his costly gifts of kindness and responding with respect and thankfulness, a wife is to gladly submit herself in every area of life.

At this point, it is important to make three biblical qualifications:

1. *Submission is always conditional upon obedience to God*—so if a husband demands that his wife disown or disobey God or commit immorality or illegality, she should not obey him (in 1 Corinthians 7 Paul permits believers to allow an unbelieving spouse to leave if they insist). If his behaviour towards her is corrupt (for example sexually degrading) or cruel (for example physically or emotionally abusive), she is not required to submit without protest to his sin, but to lovingly challenge and persuade him to change. Evangelical scholars disagree on whether sustained wickedness towards a spouse constitutes grounds for divorce. Probably the best view is that, in addition to sexual adultery, permanent abandonment or extreme cruelty is a form of unfaithfulness that destroys the

fundamental relational nature of a covenant and permits divorce, just as the LORD describes Israel's persistent rebellion as breaking their covenant relationship (Hosea 8:1), which was followed by his legal divorce (Jeremiah 3:8).

2. *Submission is not mindless.* In the Garden of Gethsemane, Jesus prayed with great passion to his Father for permission to avoid the suffering of the cross, but his concluding commitment was: "Yet not what I will, but what you will" (Mark 14:36). To submit is not to become a doormat, unable to offer an opinion or express disagreement with a husband's view. But the bottom line, after all the debate, is to submit to the leadership of her husband.

3. *Submission is not about ability, but order.* Obviously, a wife will often be more competent in some matters, or wiser in her judgements, or right on an issue. If her husband has any sense, he will listen to her opinions and delegate to her responsibilities and decisions for which she is better suited than he. But he must bear the ultimate responsibility in the marriage. A godly wife will try to trust her husband to lead her in the way God wants her to go, and let him lead and make decisions for them both, even though he is bound to make mistakes and may find the responsibility onerous.

> God's word does not leave marriages to become a battle between a man's bicep and a woman's tongue.

Such Christ-like submission, often summarised in a bride's wedding vow to love and obey (or submit to) her husband, has three major benefits:

1. *Submission fosters agreement rather than struggle.* Instead of leaving marriages in confusion that too often becomes a battle between the strength of a man's bicep and the sharpness of a woman's tongue, God has provided for a consistently loving

leadership and sensible submission in marriage that fits the way he has designed us differently as males and females. There is no justification in the Bible for any condescending sexism or boorish male domination. But the Bible does claim that, however loudly our culture recoils from recognising gender differences, God has generally designed men and women to reflect different, and complementary, and equally admirable aspects of his own character. In general, God has created women with increased capacities for his work of sacrificial support and nurture, and has created men with increased capacities for his work of protective leadership. Of course, the details of how this is worked out in a marriage will vary hugely across history, culture, personality and circumstances.

2. *Submission is attractive to unbelieving husbands.* Peter encourages Christian wives of unbelieving husbands to submit to them in confidence that their own godliness will help win their husbands to Christ (1 Peter 3:1-6). A believing wife will inevitably feel alone in spiritual matters without a believing husband to lead her, but she mustn't feel guilty for being unable to participate in the life of a church as fully as wives of believers because her husband wants her elsewhere. The Spirit of God will help believing wives to be more loving than before they were converted, and many husbands are brought to Christ through the prayers and witness of their wives.

3. *Submission will be blessed and rewarded by Christ in heaven.* Even when godly submission is unappreciated by a husband and even mocked by family and friends on earth, our Lord Jesus has been the suffering servant who knows how hard it can be to submit to others, and will surely reward the wife who submits to her husband for her Lord's sake (especially when her husband is being a thoughtless fool).

Notice that submission and love are not conditional upon each other. A godly wife will submit to her husband even when there is little wisdom to respect or enjoy. And a godly husband must love his wife even when she struggles with this issue and only rarely submits to his leadership. Each should not have to earn from the other the submissive support and the loving leadership that God wants, though it is obviously easier for a wife to submit to a loving husband, and easier for a husband to lead a respectful wife.

Submission isn't easy and requires swimming against the flow of Western culture today. But it's made a lot easier for wives when they read of the sacrificial love that the apostle will now require of husbands. If you think Paul expects a lot from wives, wait until you read what he says to their husbands!

Questions for reflection

1. What is different between the biblical understanding of what submission is, and your society's? What is similar?

2. If you are a wife, when do you find it hardest to submit? Why? How can you reflect on the gospel in such a way that you are enabled to submit willingly, rather than grudgingly?

3. If you are married, do you talk to others about your spouse only in positive, loyal ways?

PART TWO

A Word to Husbands

"Husbands, love your wives…" (Ephesians **5:25**). Strikingly, husbands are not instructed to rule or lead their wives… but to love them! Their leadership must flow from their love. Indeed, this command is repeated three times—requiring a sustained commitment of a husband's will to love his wife sacrificially by serving her through leading her. Paul offers two models for a husband's love, and both are extremely demanding:

1. *Love her "as Christ loved the church"* (**v 25**). This is required of us all back in verse 2, but here, especially of husbands for their wives: "… just as Christ loved the church and gave himself up for her" (**v 25**). A husband should take the initiative in sacrificially giving himself to the good of his wife. Loving like Christ means giving up his life even unto death; and until that is necessary, it means dying to what is easiest for him in countless little ways—perhaps helping her with domestic chores, adapting his social or sporting commitments, helping more with the children… as well as spiritual initiatives like reading the Bible with the family at the dinner table or praying with his wife as they go to sleep. A husband is to love his wife for better, for worse; for richer, for poorer; in sickness and in health—not just providing for her materially but giving himself to her physically, emotionally and spiritually. And if his career, or even his church ministry, is consistently making this impossible, then he should consider changing it for the sake of his wife.

   The aim of a godly husband's love is his wife's best interests, which Paul explains from three aspects of Christ's love. First, Christ died to make his people "holy" (**v 26**)—devoted to God. Second, he died to "cleanse" us from sin, through the spiritual washing of the word of the gospel; and third, he died to present us to himself on the last day as "radiant" in the spiritual glory of Christ (**v 27**)— without any stain of sin or wrinkle of ungodliness or blemish of imperfection, but holy and blameless in spiritual beauty.

And this, says Paul, is to be a husband's chief goal for his wife. A husband is to be concerned, not primarily for his wife's short-term happiness (perhaps hoping for an easier life himself), but for her long-term holiness, cleansing and radiance in Christ. Actually, her increasing holiness will include an increasing contentedness, and a husband who will not gently resist his wife's sin isn't loving her. He needs to be primarily concerned for the day when she will stand before Christ; and her spiritual condition will be taken into account when he stands before Christ himself.

A Christian husband will want to support Christ's will for his wife, not with an overly intense marriage, but with one that enables them to serve God together and so proclaim the triumph of Christ in the spiritual realms. Even if he is recently converted, perhaps long after his wife, he should try to learn to pray for her and with her—for her needs as well as his own.

> A husband is to be concerned not primarily for his wife's short-term happiness but for her long-term holiness.

He'll want to enable her love of Jesus to grow through attendance together at church, an appropriate small group and in private devotions. And a godly man will find the growing godliness of his wife beautiful at every age. All of this is hugely challenging, but in Christ there is never-ending forgiveness for our failures and strength to keep trying.

2. *Love her as your own body* (**v 28**). Paul offers a second model for a husband's love: "In this same way, husbands ought to love their wives as their own bodies. He who loves his wife loves himself. After all, no one ever hated their own body, but they feed and care for their body, just as Christ does the church—for we are members of his body" (**v 28-30**). Paul endorses the teaching of Genesis and Jesus, that in marriage a man and a woman are united as two

persons in one body, which is expressed in sexual intercourse. So just as any sensible person provides for their own body, a husband will take responsibility for cherishing his wife, seeing that she has all she needs. This doesn't necessarily mean that a husband must earn all or most of the salary, but it is primarily his responsibility to ensure proper provision for his wife and children—not to satisfy her demands or to match extravagant friends, but for her sustained welfare, and especially spiritually.

Again, how a husband loves his wife will vary hugely from marriage to marriage. It is probably helpful to observe that each partner has a different "love language"—the way in which we each long to experience love—which is often shaped by our upbringing as much as our personality. We often naively assume that this will be the way that our spouse also wants to experience our love. But since we're all very different, it's important for a couple to try to discuss how they each like to be shown love. In *The Five Love Languages*, Gary Chapman suggests five different "languages" by which we commonly long for expressions of love:

1. Touch (including, but not exclusively, sexually)

2. Words of affection (usually affirmation and encouragement or intimacy)

3. Gifts (especially unexpected)

4. Time (to talk, or perhaps not to talk but to share an activity or inactivity)

5. Actions (kindnesses of every kind and especially sex)

In the context of a sexually super-heated Western culture, a Christian couple may find two principles for expectations of sexual intimacy to be helpful: the partner who desires more sexual activity may need to recognise that their spouse is offering all they can as the person they are in their circumstances and season of life; and the partner who is more reluctant may need to remember that in getting married, they were promising to do their best to serve their spouse sexually.

United Together

Paul next reminds his readers of the teaching of Genesis, repeated by Jesus, regarding the unity of a marriage which illustrates Christ's love for us: "For this reason a man will leave his father and mother and be united to his wife, and the two will become one flesh" (**v 31**). As we have noted before, Paul's teaching is that as part of God's "very good" creation (Paul is quoting from the creation account in Genesis 2:24), God has decreed that a marriage creates a new family. This means that a husband and wife are to make each other their first priority, ahead of parents and other members of their wider family (which can be difficult in many cultures). The husband and wife are united (but not fused), meaning joined together in a partnership of body (expressed sexually), mind (expressed in conversation), and soul (expressed in a spiritual union recognised by God).

This means that, except for unfaithfulness (adultery and sustained abandonment or cruelty), divorce is forbidden by God. This teaching (following Jesus in Matthew 19:1-12) contrasts starkly with the morality of Western societies today. At present in Britain, half of those who marry will end up divorced, about 120,000 marriages end in divorce each year, and the average marriage now lasts 11.4 years. But apart from the misery that divorce usually brings upon those who divorce, the hurt inflicted on any children is immeasurable; on nearly all social indicators, the children of married parents perform better than those who are not living with married parents. These facts have caused Sir Paul Coleridge, a British High Court judge with 40 years' experience in the Family Division, to observe: "Marriage and family breakdown is one of the most destructive scourges of our time".

The relief of the gospel is that although almost everyone who has been married has been emotionally, if not physically, unfaithful, and no wife or husband has ever loved their spouse as God commands, we can all come to him for his complete forgiveness and for the transforming power of his Holy Spirit to help us become better wives and husbands. Marriages in churches are all under differing degrees of strain—and, despite the impression we often give on Sunday mornings, no marriage is without its difficulties and regrets. But God enables a patient forgiveness and gradual change that goes far beyond what is possible without God. Gospel-driven forgiveness is the glue that sticks our imperfect marriages together—gradually overcoming bitterness and despair with real hope and joy.

It's Not About Your Marriage!

But at the end of this passage about marriage, we discover that Paul's deeper focus here is not upon our marital happiness at all! He says: "I am talking about Christ and the church" (Ephesians **5:32**). The "profound mystery" here is not marriage itself. It is the "mystery" (meaning "revealed secret") of the gospel, which he clarified earlier in the letter: namely, that people of every background are being reconciled to God and each other through the death of Christ, to manifest God's triumphant wisdom over destructive evil powers, in the spiritual realms in his church.

So, the "one flesh" union of a Christian marriage under Christ, between two people who may be incredibly different from each other, is a powerful demonstration in the spiritual realms of the wisdom of God's eternal plan to unite everything under Christ! The power of the gospel to motivate a Christian wife to submissively support her husband, and to motivate a Christian husband to sacrificially love his wife, despite their sins and their differences, provides a powerful witness in our earthly churches of the victory of God over destructive evil powers. To put this simply, if God can keep Christians together in marriage, it's obvious that his eternal plan is working!

Genesis 2 presents marriage as the union of a man and woman, reflecting the unity of God; the Song of Songs describes the erotic passion of a husband and wife, reflecting the intimate love of Christ for his people; Psalm 45 celebrates the royal magnificence of a king who makes a poor girl his princess, as Christ has accepted the church as his bride; Revelation 7 and 21 celebrate the multicultural diversity of Jesus' church at his wedding banquet. But here in Ephesians 5, Paul celebrates marriage as a powerful illustration of the sacrificial love of Christ and the joyful submission of his church—as a spectacular witness to God's gospel plan in the spiritual realms.

So if we struggle to understand how Christ loves us—think of an utterly devoted husband. If we struggle to understand how to please Jesus—think of a beautifully supportive wife. And if we're single, widowed or divorced, we mustn't miss where Paul directs our attention—not towards human marriage, but towards the marriage of Christ and his church, which every believer can look forward to.

Equally, if we're married and painfully aware that our marriage is far from ideal, we must remember that it can only ever be a shadow of our future marriage made in heaven, when we shall all be united with Christ at the most glorious wedding banquet, to enjoy a never-ending honeymoon in the new-creation paradise, and experience perfect marital bliss for ever! None of us will miss out. We will all experience intimate and ecstatic satisfaction in our union with Christ in eternity. And when our marriages are struggling, while we stay together we are not a battlefield but a victory parade, demonstrating God's power to keep us together under Christ, an illustration of the gospel; for the Bible is the story of God choosing a wife for his Son—and, astonishingly, choosing wretched sinners like us to be that bride, and so to enjoy his marvellous grace. Our happy marriage to Christ is the goal of history; and every earthly marriage, whether as a beautiful comparison or an ugly contrast, is a powerful reminder of it.

> A struggling marriage that stays together is not a battleground but a victory parade of God's power.

So to summarise, Paul says with economical brevity that "each one of you also must love his wife as he loves himself, and the wife must respect her husband" (**v 33**)—because your marriage is a vital part of the picture that your church is painting in the spiritual realms, of the union of Christ and his church!

Questions for reflection

1. How is the Bible's view of what leadership means different from your society's?

2. If you are a husband, in what ways are you leading your wife in a Christ-like way? In what ways is the Spirit prompting you to be more Christ-like?

3. If you are unhappily unmarried, or unhappily married, how do verses 31-32 help you not to make too much of human marriage? Are you in any danger of failing to enjoy the greater relationship (between Christ and the church) because you do not enjoy the picture of that relationship (human marriage)?

11. AT HOME AND AT WORK

God is a "family of three"—so he designed us for family life, in our homes and in our churches. God is also a creative "worker"—so he designed us for creative work, in our employment and in our gospel ministry.

As humanity continues to rebel against our Creator's principles for families and for work, we will find that our homes and workplaces often become the scenes of our most obvious failings and flaws. They can become not only dysfunctional but also deeply unhappy places. So when Christ took flesh to save us, by living our Christian life for us, he was born into the family of a workman to live perfectly by the principles of our Creator. And when he died in our place for our sins, he was punished for all our weakness and wickedness, at home and at work, so that we can be forgiven and seek his strength to change.

This passage provides some very simple principles for life under Christ at home and at work. It was written for the Christian churches in first-century Turkey, when family life and business life were largely conducted from the same extended household. But the principles are intentionally timeless, because Paul is still explaining what it means for God's people, in every place and age, to "be filled with the Spirit" and "submit to one another" (5:18, 21). For God's eternal plan—to unite all things under Christ (1:10) to demonstrate his triumphant wisdom in the heavenly realms in his church (3:10)—is evident not only when we gather in our congregations or engage in gospel ministry, but also in our obedience to Christ in our families and workplaces. So, our homes and offices are as much a place of worship of God as any church building or mission event!

In this passage, each member of an extended household is being addressed, because in Christ, everyone has equal dignity and importance. In the last chapter we looked at Paul's guidance for wives and husbands. Now he turns to consider children and fathers, then slaves and masters. He begins with the youngest…

Children: Obey your Parents

Paul begins by addressing "children" (**6:1**). The word used here for children is actually not about age but relationship. But the context of discipline and instruction makes clear that Paul has in mind pre-adult children who are unmarried and still living at home. The command to honour our father and mother (Exodus 20:12; Matthew 5:17) is for all of life, but its practice will clearly adapt as we get older, and as the needs of parents change.

Paul tells children to "obey your parents" (Ephesians **6:1**)—this command requires children to fully comply with their parents' instructions. This is obviously easier when those instructions are sensible and clearly explained, and when the children have reason to trust that their parents love them. But children are naturally as sinful as their parents, and so they need both tons of disciplined love (not indulgence) *and* loving discipline (not bullying). It is a sobering comment upon Western society that so many parents complain that they can't discipline their unruly children; for Paul writes elsewhere of disobedient children being characteristic of pagan depravity (Romans 1:30) and of the evil of the last days before Christ returns (2 Timothy 3:2).

> Our children need disciplined love and loving discipline—not indulgence or bullying.

Paul here provides children with spiritual motivation for their obedience: to obey "in the Lord, for this is right" (Ephesians **6:1**). Children don't have to obey parents because parents are more important than children (they aren't), but as part of a child's loving obedience to Christ. Within the limits of living for the Lord (not complying with immoral, idolatrous or anti-gospel requirements such as being forbidden to pray or follow Jesus), this command makes obeying parents not just the most peaceful thing to do, but the morally right thing to do. As a child clears the dishes or tidies their bedroom or comes home before midnight and struggles to understand why this is such a big deal for their parents, they don't have to believe that their parents know best (they often don't); nor accept that a cleared table or clean bedroom is morally superior (it isn't). They just need to remember that obeying their parents is the right thing because Jesus has asked them to do it, and that these are opportunities to please their Saviour. It is obviously helpful when a Christian parent can find an opportunity to explain this to their child.

Paul explains that such obedience is right, not because society thinks so (ours is increasingly confused about this issue) but as part of a wider attitude: "Honour your father and mother" (**v 2**). This is the fifth of the ten summary commandments to Israel in Exodus 20 and Deuteronomy 5—it matters. Indeed, in Scripture the command to honour our parents is treated as seriously as idolatry. This is because the relationship of a parent and child is, after marriage, the most powerful illustration of the loving relationship between God and his people. The word "honour" means serious respect and is commonly translated "fear" or "reverence". For adults, this means respecting our parents' wisdom by seeking and heeding their advice; it will mean caring for them by visiting, providing practical care and financial help, and possibly accommodating them as they become frailer, and more unwell and afraid. Just as we will not allow our kids to disrespect our spouse, we must not disrespect our own parents or parents-in-law in the way we talk about them.

Again, Paul gives children a motivation for obedience. This command has a clear promise attached to it: "that it may go well with you and that you may enjoy long life on the earth" (Ephesians **6:3**). In this quotation, Paul has dropped the Old Testament reference to life in the promised land (Exodus 20:12, Deuteronomy 5:16), because he understands that God has already kept his promise of life in the earthly kingdom, in the prosperity of Israel. He is saying that for Christians today, honouring our parents is part of our allegiance to Christ and will be rewarded by God in the coming kingdom of heaven, and to some degree in the fullness of life now (though qualified by our sin and the corruption of this world). Christians who honour their parents will tend to know the joys of a close family in which children ordinarily respect their parents.

Fathers: Nurture your Children

Now, in verse 4, Paul turns to fathers. He says simply: "Fathers, do not exasperate your children; instead, bring them up in the training and instruction of the Lord" (**v 4**). Each word is carefully chosen…

"Fathers"—as heads of families, dads have a special responsibility (and single or neglected mothers will have to fill in for a father's absence). Although wives may have more time with the children than their husbands can, dads still have a primary responsibility, which they shouldn't neglect (so mothers able to stay at home can greatly help dads by deferring important decisions until there's a chance to discuss the issues with their husbands). Paul gives fathers a negative instruction followed by a positive one.

First, don't "exasperate your children". Fathers shouldn't provoke their children to anger with severe or relentless discipline, unreasonably harsh demands, inconsistent or unfair rules, constant criticism or humiliation, or insensitivity to different seasons of a child's weaknesses, fears and needs. I've annoyed my kids most when I've failed to think into their world with empathy—for example, forgetting how each child is a different character with unique needs and ways of expressing themselves. When they're young, it's easy to forget that "naughtiness" is often frustration caused by parents. And when they're teenagers, it's tempting to harass them about their untidy rooms, music volume, TV-show choices or social life, when many of these issues are really cultural rather than moral. The old advice about "taming the will without crushing the spirit" is as important as ever. So perhaps the best antidote to exasperating our children, whether difficult toddlers or grumpy teenagers, is consciously to resolve to enjoy them as precious gifts from God—to recall that we were all kids once, and to remember how patient our heavenly Father has been with us when we were defiant and grumpy!

> The best antidote to exasperating our children is to resolve to enjoy them as precious gifts from God.

Second comes the positive: do "bring them up in the training and instruction of the Lord". The words "bring them up" mean to nourish or nurture children. This implies long-term relational care and not rapid mechanistic results. It's amazing how a monstrous four-year old who is consistently loved and disciplined can become a charming young adult by their late teens.

The word "training" means corrective discipline. Discipline certainly includes correcting behaviour with firm words and actions. As a father of four great children said to our church about parenting toddlers:

> "You must win that battle of wills, or your child will grow up to find it impossible to take direction from a teacher or employer, and impossible to accept the critique of the Bible at church—you must win that battle!"

There is, of course, a massive difference between children being childish (which loving parents will tolerate patiently) and disobedient (which loving parents will not); and also a big difference between a child's spirited energy (which needs to be encouraged) and a child's stubborn wilfulness (which needs to be tamed).

As a father of five myself, I don't believe that references to not "sparing the rod" in Proverbs necessarily require corporal punishment.

But they do require some suitably unpleasant deterrence of disobedience, whether being removed from a situation to sit in disgrace on the stairs, or withdrawing a mobile phone or other privilege. If Christian parents do propose smacking, it should surely be carefully considered (not reactive anger), extremely restrained (not leaving marks), and demonstrably restorative (not pointless or confusing). We need to retain our confidence that it's loving to provide consistent discipline, just as our heavenly Father promises to discipline his spiritual children as proof of his love (Hebrews 12:4-11), because children need clear boundaries.

But correcting behaviour is only part of what Paul is talking about... More important than behavioural discipline is training the attitudes of our children—which results in their behaviour. This brings us to Bible teaching. Godly dads will be trying to make time at home to read the Bible and discuss how to apply biblical principles to daily life, and for quality conversations to happen naturally. It's been helpfully said that no one on his deathbed ever regretted spending too little time in the office!

The words "instruction of the Lord" here have the comprehensive sense of both parenting in a Christian manner and teaching them the Christian faith. To this end, surely the three biggest things we can do are:

1. stay married (or pursue peace with their other parent if we're not married to them) and be there for our children as far as is possible, especially at key moments;

2. love our spouse well, for children learn what loving faithfulness looks like from us; and...

3. take our children to a good church in a committed rather than casual way—a church where the gospel of grace (and not just rules about not kissing or smoking) is taught to kids from the Bible, accompanied by lots of fun.

We need to partner with our church's children's and youth leaders—but not entirely delegate our responsibilities to them. We will probably want to avoid the guilt-inducing advice of those who boast about their marvellous techniques for manufacturing ideal children (sadly, there is sometimes posturing among wealthy evangelical parents that only thinly disguises a rather worldly idolatry of their children). There can be no doubt that at all stages of parenting, the single most important thing we can give our kids is a loving home, with all the crazy laughter that the security of the gospel provides. However, many parents who feel confident when their children are young and compliant, understandably feel overwhelmed by huge anxieties when their kids become teenagers struggling with alcohol, pornography, drugs and the immorality of their friends at school or in the neighbourhood. Though often frightening and certainly humbling, such challenges can be big opportunities for parents to learn to pray and trust our Lord, and for our teenagers to discover that we will always love them, however much parents and teenagers get frustrated with each other.

Some helpful suggestions emerging from the families at our church over the years include:

- being brave about discussing our children's challenges with older Christians and church leaders.

- reading a children's Bible and praying individually with small kids when they go to bed.

- reading the Bible as a family at the tea table when the kids are school-age, even if the kids complain loudly about homework. If we take turns to read a short passage, keep discussions brief, and pray about what we've learned, we can demonstrate that God is real, important and loving.

- praying about daily stuff: responding to successes and crises and birthdays and exams with prayer, which powerfully models ordinary living by faith.

- periodically taking each of the kids for a private catch-up over a drink, as a great opportunity to listen carefully and catch up on the spiritual realities of the lives of our kids, and to offer some help and prayer.

Three Essentials for Raising Children

It may be helpful to remember three things:

1. It takes a church to raise kids—so turn up! They will need spiritually healthy role models other than their parents, for them to aspire to emulate. So take them to church and, where possible, to a church summer camp. Children are saved by God's grace and not by our good parenting—but putting our kids under credible Bible-teaching is far more valuable than swimming or tennis lessons. But don't completely delegate your parental responsibility to others—a little encouragement in the faith from dad or mum means more than a lot from the youth leaders.

2. It takes the gospel to raise kids—so speak up! Let's talk about the kindness of God's forgiving grace—and not just about God's laws—including age-appropriate apologies to them for our sins and errors (though not so much that it undermines their security in us). And it's important to share what we understand as well as what we find confusing about God's love—for example, when he doesn't give us what we pray for, or when we are coping with disappointment or suffering in the family. Hard times are when our kids are listening most carefully.

3. It takes God to raise kids—so pray up! It was the big thing my parents did for their five kids; and we can all do this for our own kids, and the children in our church family. Children united by the gospel under the rule of Christ are as much part of God's plan to display his grace in the heavenly realms as anyone else in our church.

If you have children, they will probably take it in turns to make you sick with worry, even after they leave home. But you can pray for them every night, knowing that God loves them even more than you do and that our heavenly Father understands children and wants to help us all to bring them up well. So we can resolve to enjoy parenting at every stage, in all its exhausting complexity, confident that God will help us—because a family gathered under Christ is proclaiming Christ's victory over evil in the heavenly realms!

Questions for reflection

This is a very practical passage. So...

1. How will you better honour your parents?

2. How will you better raise your children and/or support others in doing so?

3. How does the gospel—the truths that we are all sinful, but can all be saved, by God's grace alone—help you cope with the hard parts of parenting, and remain humble when you know success in parenting?

PART TWO

Working for the Boss

Now Paul turns to focus upon the household employment situation of slaves and their masters to clarify some principles that, despite huge differences of social context, remain hugely relevant for our working lives today.

"Slaves, obey your earthly masters with respect and fear, and with sincerity of heart, just as you would obey Christ" (Ephesians **6:5**). Slavery was a foundational part of the economy and society of the Roman Empire and the whole ancient world. It was generally practised humanely in households, but as it is contrary to Christian principles of human dignity, Paul encourages Philemon to accept Onesimus no longer as a slave but as a brother in Christ (Philemon 16-17). Throughout the Bible, God provides realistic principles that will soften the recurring evils of slavery in every age. It was therefore evangelical Christians, like William Wilberforce, who worked tirelessly for the abolition of the slave trade in Britain; and the civil rights campaigner Martin Luther King was clearly driven by his Christian principles.

Here, however, Paul is not trying to stir up a social-reform campaign, but directly addressing the slaves in the church in the reality of their daily struggles. It is worth noting that such advice was a dignity without precedent in Roman society, for these slaves now enjoyed equality in church with their owners! But their spiritual freedom in Christ was not matched by their social conditions. Paul provides a longer section for slaves than for masters, offering them many encouragements that reflect the challenge they faced to remain godly when being mistreated. Tragically today, there remains a great deal of slavery, especially in the wickedness of sex-slave trafficking (even in Britain); moreover, despite the work of Christians and others in establishing trade unions and legislation protecting workers and children from abuse, much employment in and on behalf of Western nations remains to some degree exploitative and even abusive. So there is still much to be learned here by all working Christians. Of course, in many other countries, slavery is still a dreadful normality. Paul gives three clear principles for worshipping Christ in our working lives:

First, Christian slaves and employees should "obey" the instructions we are given by our bosses (Ephesians **6:5**). Such obedience is always within the three main biblical boundaries—that the instructions are:

- not immoral—the Hebrew midwives would not obey their Egyptian masters in killing baby boys (Exodus 1), just as Christian doctors and nurses will not collude in abortions.

- not idolatrous—in Babylon, the young Jewish exiles, Shadrach, Meshach and Abednego, wouldn't worship the emperor's statue (Daniel 3), just as Christians will not participate in multi-faith services.

- not suppressing the gospel—the apostles would not obey the instructions of the Sanhedrin Council to stop preaching salvation through Christ (Acts 4), just as Christians cannot agree to be silenced from speaking about Christ (especially if it isn't hindering our fulfilment of the duties for which we are employed). We can remain wisely quiet but we cannot deny Christ or be permanently silenced, but must take up our cross and not be ashamed of Christ or his gospel (Mark 8:34-38).

Within these principles we can accept the direction of our employers because all authorities are appointed by God (Romans 13:1). If our employers (or the government) threaten to punish our faithful witness, then we are free to witness and then accept punishment or seek legal redress (as Paul did in appealing to Roman law in Acts 22:25), or where possible find another job and count it a privilege to be persecuted. Christians will not refuse obedience to our bosses merely because we feel tired, unfairly treated or demeaned, for we do our work for Christ, who suffered much worse in saving us. We are to obey out of our "respect" (deference), "fear" (reverence) and with "sincerity" (openness) before God (Ephesians **6:5**). In other words, our earthly masters may be utterly undeserving, but in our hearts our work for them is also done for Christ.

There is no divide between "sacred" ministry (in the church) and "secular" ministry (in the world). We worship our Lord wherever we are, being holy in all of our lives—and so we obey the instructions of our masters as coming from God's appointed authority. We obey, not as a show for personal advancement, "to win their favour" (Ephesians **6:6**); for instance, by leaving a jacket over the chair to pretend we're still in the office, or claiming the work of others as our own, or attending to lots of personal administration during working hours. Rather, we are to obey our bosses as slaves of the Christ who served us as our slave by dying for us, and still serves us as our advocate before the Father. We are prepared to serve others in our work as part of doing "the will of God" from our hearts (**v 6**).

> Our masters may be undeserving, but in our hearts our work for them is also done for Christ.

I heard recently of a currency-broking firm in London where the senior executives were mocking the faith of some senior and junior Christian employees. But when one cynical director heard the names of the believers, he conceded: "Well, I have to admit they make good workers!" That kind of witness at work gains a hearing for the gospel.

But why are we to work like this? Because, second, we are "serving the Lord, not people" (**v 7**). Since the whole earth belongs to the living God, who provides our daily needs, when we contribute to the farming business or IT company we work for, in a small way we are helping to govern God's creation. Although no business is purely motivated or practised (and we should choose more ethical businesses if we can), we can serve our earthly masters wholeheartedly, knowing that other employees, and consumers and clients, will benefit. We're "serving the Lord" and not just the boss.

As workers, we are one part of the means by which our loving Creator provides for the daily needs of the world (however inequitably world leaders are distributing its resources). Whether we write contracts or computer software or sermons, fix pipes or broken arms or trucks, or wash the family laundry, dirty windows or pots in a restaurant, we worship God when we do it for him. For we write, fix and wash to feed the family, and to earn money to contribute to the gospel work of our church, and to seek opportunities to witness to our fellow workers, and to please the big boss, Jesus, enthroned in heaven.

And, third, as we work like this, "the Lord will reward each one for whatever good they do" (**v 8**). Even though an earthly master may not notice or care what we do, or may be biased or miserly in how they reward us, our Lord sees everything, including the motives for doing it, and will delight to reward us in heaven. Whether we're slaves or masters, on a high salary or a minimum wage, whatever our company position or social status, Christ will generously reward good works done for him with a bonus in heaven among "the incomparable riches of his grace" (2:7). For, "we are God's handiwork, created in Christ Jesus to do good works, which God prepared in advance for us to do" (2:10).

This emphasis upon serving the Lord wholeheartedly in our work raises the issue of whether those who could work for the gospel in church should do so. In most situations, giving up a normal job to re-train for serving the gospel of God as a missionary, evangelist, church planter, pastor, youth worker or church administrator will involve considerable sacrifice. The Bible teaches that we all have a creation ministry serving God in responsibly harvesting and developing this earth; and that every believer also has a new-creation gospel ministry seeking opportunities to explain the gospel, which can save people from hell for heaven for eternity. Both are godly ministries, but Jesus made gospel ministry his priority, because the forgiveness of sins is our greatest human need.

We should all do the same—that is, as the people we are, with the gifts and opportunities that God has given us, we should all maximise our gospel ministry. For most of us, that will mean worshipping God by working wholeheartedly in the garage or bank or school where we work, living godly lives that commend the gospel, and taking every opportunity to explain it to our colleagues. We may be the only Christians they can ever get to know. And we will also earn money to finance gospel work in our church and in all kinds of mission, near and far. But some who are gifted and available for more gospel ministry can be set free from earning a living in order to maximise their gospel work. All Christians are gospel ministers, committed in every way we can be to maximising gospel ministry, for the saving and gathering into Christ's church of many, to the glory of God!

Working as the Boss

And now for the bosses: "Masters, treat your slaves in the same way. Do not threaten them, since you know that he who is both their Master and yours is in heaven, and there is no favouritism with him" (**6:9**).

"Masters" were regarded as owning their slaves. But Paul does not neglect them because of the sinful institution they served. The wealthy and powerful must serve Christ as wholeheartedly as the poor. He issues a culturally shocking instruction to all masters: treat your slaves in the same way that you would like to be treated yourself! And this principle extends to anyone in authority in the workplace today.

This doesn't mean abdicating the role of leadership, or the responsibility to direct the workforce—leadership is a ministry of service, as we see most clearly in Jesus (and many businesses and churches suffer from a chronic lack of leadership ministry). Masters mustn't abdicate their leadership, or there will be chaos in the workplace from which nobody benefits! But it does mean treating slaves and employees with exactly the same respect, fear and sincerity for

Christ as the slaves should show in obeying them. A master like that is rare indeed!

This requires masters then, and employers now, not to threaten their employees with unjust or arbitrary consequences. There will need to be codes of conduct, discipline and penalties, but also grievance procedures and independent arbitration, not terrified workers living in fear of their boss unjustly taking their livelihoods. Paul says this is for two reasons. First, Christian bosses know that their own heavenly Master is also their employees' heavenly Master! They are accountable to the same Lord, who will judge their work impartially. Clearly, if we neglect or mistreat our employees, we risk facing his loving discipline now and receiving reduced rewards in heaven.

Second, God doesn't show any favouritism. Those who are in senior positions may be used to social privileges and advantages within the company and in the wider world—but there is no social bias with God! He will not be swayed to reward bosses more in heaven because of their better education or expensive suits! He is not interested in the many gifts and opportunities that the middle classes can take because they are privileged, since he gave them all! If masters are used to preferential treatment now, we need to know that it will not be like that in eternity. CEOs and street-sweepers will stand in the same dock on judgment day. To be saved, but received into a heaven with muted praise from our Lord

> CEOs and street-sweepers will stand in the same dock on judgment day.

amid the deafening silence of a disgusted heavenly crowd, because we were harsh and unsympathetic to our employees, is not a happy prospect! Christian bosses must be firm but fair, unafraid of necessary discipline, but never dismissive of workers' needs, or miserly in paying them properly because they lack options or a voice. As the Lord himself told his disciples: "You know that those who are regarded as rulers of the Gentiles lord it over them ... Not so with you ... For even the Son of Man did not come to be served, but to serve, and to give his life as a ransom for many" (Mark 10:42-43, 45).

Displaying God's Triumph, Monday to Saturday

In this wonderfully practical passage, masters, slaves, fathers and children are all encouraged to live and work together as servants of Christ, to demonstrate in the heavenly realms the triumphant wisdom of God in his eternal mission of gathering us under the rule of Christ. For the triumphant victory of the cross over evil powers is not only demonstrated in church on Sundays; it is powerfully displayed when Christians from every background submit to the rule of Christ in our homes and workplaces from Monday to Saturday as well. And although our homes and workplaces can be painful and difficult because of sin, our churches can provide us with an encouraging foretaste of the happy family life and satisfying creative workplace that Christians will enjoy in the coming kingdom of God.

Questions for reflection

1. How are you tempted to be a people-pleaser in the workplace (or anywhere else)? Why is it so appealing?

2. What would change if you remembered that you can always, and should always, be seen by and be pleasing to your Father?

3. If you have responsibility for or authority over others in your workplace, how much and how consciously is your leadership modelled on Christ's? How could you reflect the Son of Man's character better?

12. STAND FIRM IN THE FIGHT

Now Paul reaches the dramatic finale to his letter: "Finally, be strong in the Lord and in his mighty power. Put on the full armour of God, so that you can take your stand against the devil's schemes" (**v 10-11**).

He begins "Finally" because, far from being a random diversion or disconnected afterthought, this passage is actually the glorious climax to Ephesians—and it is all about spiritual warfare. Paul outlines God's battle-plan for our spiritual resistance to the devil's scheming: he locates our unlimited supplies in God; he analyses the threat of the enemy forces to divide and conquer us; he clarifies our response in standing firm; he trains us in wearing the protective armour we will need; and then explains his strategy for victory... namely, praying for world mission.

The Devil Today

For many Western Christians, such talk of struggling with satanic powers sounds suspiciously extreme, even crazy. We need to understand a little about spiritual warfare.

Christians are called to peace with God and other people. Jesus said: "Blessed are the peacemakers ... love your enemies and pray for those who persecute you" (Matthew 5:9, 44). So Christians condemn the misguided violence of the Crusades as much as the Islamic *jihad* of today. But Christians are called to a spiritual battle: to "fight the good fight of the faith" (1 Timothy 6:12). This is our spiritual struggle to maintain our faith in the gospel of God against the opposition of the world, the flesh and the devil. We wrestle with the arguments of the world when "we demolish arguments and every pretension that sets itself up against the knowledge of God" with the truth of the gospel (2 Corinthians 10:5). We kill off the corruptions of our flesh when "by the Spirit [we] put to death the misdeeds of the body" (Romans 8:13) with obedience to the gospel. And, as we shall now see, we resist the schemes of the devil when we "put on the full armour of God" (Ephesians **6:11**). The Ephesians had evidently grown up in an extremely superstitious culture, terrified of Satan and demonic powers. Paul wanted his readers, then and now, to understand spiritual warfare from a biblical perspective. Here are five key biblical principles:

■ *Satan is a real and vicious enemy of God and his people.* Some of us are dangerously oblivious to satanic powers, because we're influenced by the **rationalistic** materialism of our culture. The Bible says Satan is real—a rebellious angel, hurled down from heaven and "filled with fury, because he knows that his time is short", who "leads the whole world astray" and is the "father of lies" because he has lost all grip on reality (Revelation 12:12, 9; John 8:44). There is, however, the opposite risk of becoming dangerously obsessed with spiritual warfare and far too afraid of Satan. In London, for instance, there have been dreadful reports of children being brutally tortured by misguided churches attempting **exorcisms** because they don't understand how the deliverance ministry of Christ operates through the gospel. And best-selling authors continue exploiting those who are poorly taught with misleading novels about spiritual warfare. Many Christians need to understand that "the reason the Son of God appeared was to destroy the devil's work" (1 John 3:8).

■ *Satan tempts us to doubt God's word.* From the beginning, Satan's essential strategy has been to tempt us to doubt God's word—to distrust its clarity, truth and goodness. Swirling around in our minds, therefore, we'll hear his familiar temptations to question Scripture: "Did God really say" *you must not satisfy your desires in that way? "You will not certainly die"* and be punished for this action or lifestyle... *"Your eyes will be opened, and you will be like God"* if you make up your own rules *(Genesis 3:1, 4, 5).* Like Adam and Eve, we're tempted to doubt and then disobey God's word; if it looks attractive, feels good and seems adult, we'll satisfy our appetites! Following our ancestors, we now experience pain, death and exclusion from God's paradise. Wonderfully, in the Gospels we find the Holy Spirit sending Jesus into the desert to fight with his obedient faith, on our behalf, against Satan's temptations to doubt and disobey God's

> Like Adam and Eve, if it looks attractive, feels good and seems adult, we'll satisfy our appetites.

word (Matthew 4:1-11). As our new Adam (the founder of a new humanity), he completed our Christian life—a life of faith in God's word that resists Satan's lies—perfectly for us.

■ *The Old Testament records how God rescued Israel from bondage to pagan fear.* The ancient peoples surrounding Israel were terrified of demonic spirits. They were steeped in idolatry and witchcraft, expressed in grotesque immorality and violence. God warned his people: "Let no one be found among you who ... practises divination or sorcery, interprets omens, engages in witchcraft, or casts spells, or who is a medium or spiritist or who consults the dead. Anyone who does these things is detestable to the LORD" (Deuteronomy 18:10-12). That's why Christians today organise "pumpkin parties" instead of "Halloween horrors" for their small children, and ignore the horoscopes in their newspapers (Paul warns us in 1 Timothy 4, however, that demonic teaching is also to be heard in ascetic religious rules denying the enjoyment of good gifts from our loving Creator, like marriage and food, which make God seem miserable). In 1 Samuel 28, we hear God condemning **Saul** for consulting the "medium at Endor" and raising the spirit of **Samuel**—which warns us to leave the spirits of the dead well alone. In Job 1, we read of the LORD employing Satan's cruel desire to afflict Job and tempt him to doubt God, to purify and reward Job's faith instead—so we can trust that Satan is on a short leash, completely subject to the will of our heavenly Father. And in Zechariah 3 we read of the LORD silencing Satan's accusation of Joshua the high priest, and protecting him as a forgiven sinner, like a "burning stick snatched from the fire", by clothing him in the fine robes of God's righteousness—as we all are in Christ. Strikingly, in all the Old Testament, God never identifies demons as a cause of Israel's wickedness, nor exorcism as the solution. Even the most degraded behaviour is condemned as human sin requiring repentance, and never as demons needing exorcism.

■ *In the New Testament we learn that Christ came to defeat the devil.* The gospels record Jesus' absolute power as divine King over the demons provoked by his presence. But Jesus cast out demons not with bizarre and cruel ceremonies, but by teaching the gospel. The people were amazed and said: "A new teaching—and with authority! He even gives orders to impure spirits and they obey him!" (Mark 1:27, 38-39). So today, when we preach the gospel that Jesus preached, and pray as Jesus taught us: "Deliver us from the evil one" (Matthew 6:13), God continues to deliver people from the kingdom of darkness into the kingdom of the Son he loves, driving out "the spirit who is now at work in those who are disobedient" (Ephesians 2:2). This is why our churches don't need any papal exorcists, or deliverance ministries other than prayerful gospel-teaching, for this is Christ's deliverance ministry. Indeed, Jesus explains to a hostile delegation in Mark 3:27 that his casting out of demons proved he had come to rob Satan, like a thief tying up a strong man to plunder his house. Christians are stolen goods, plundered from Satan's lair! For Christ came to die, not only to satisfy God for our sins and to provide an example of sacrificial love, but to bind Satan and deliver us from his condemnation under God's law. For when he cancelled the written code of the law by fulfilling its terms on the cross, Christ "disarmed the powers and authorities" and made a "public spectacle of them, triumphing over them by the cross" (Colossians 2:14-15). One of the most wonderful illustrations of Christ's deliverance ministry is given in his deliverance of the "Gerasene demoniac" (Mark 5:1-20). This poor man was possessed by a legion of demons and afflicted by uncontrollable aggression, restless anti-social behaviour and miserable self-harm—the demons had inflamed within him the damage of sin in us all. With a word, Jesus restored him to sit at peace, clothed with dignity, and restored to his right mind. His deliverance illustrates the ministry we all enjoy through the gospel of Christ.

■ *Ephesians teaches that Christ's conquest of Satan is displayed in his church.* But why is Paul speaking about spiritual warfare here in Ephesians 6? Because this is the hugely significant climax of this letter. It brings our responsibility, to live in unity under Christ for world mission, into the heavenly realms of spiritual warfare. Remember that Paul was writing from prison to the flagship church of Ephesus. He wrote to explain God's glorious plan to gather all things under Christ, of which his church, spiritually resurrected in union with Christ, is his showcase in the spiritual realms (chapters 1 – 3). He has explained that Christ has triumphed over Satan at the cross and has been enthroned in heaven to rule over all evil powers, "far above all rule and authority, power and dominion" (1:21). God continues to rescue people from Satan's influence, as he grants saving faith through his gospel, to those who "followed the ways of this world and of the ruler of the kingdom of the air, the spirit who is now at work in those who are disobedient" (2:2), and as he seats us in his presence with the risen Christ (v 6). God now displays the wisdom of his gospel plan to satanic powers, holding aloft his church like a trophy, "that now, through the church, the manifold wisdom of God should be made known to the rulers and authorities in the heavenly realms" (3:10). This is why church unity matters—we are not to "give the devil a foothold" (4:27) with divisions that undermine or stall our world evangelism. Paul has therefore called for his readers to maintain their unity in their earthly congregations under Christ (chapters 4 – 6). He will now complete his explanation of how God is demonstrating his Son's victory over Satan, through his churches standing firm in gospel convictions by praying for world mission.

Who we Struggle Against

"Our struggle is not against flesh and blood, but against the rulers, against the authorities, against the powers of this dark world and against the spiritual forces of evil in the heavenly realms" (**6:12**). Our "struggle" (literally "wrestle") is the vicious hand-to-hand combat of our personal faith in the gospel, not a disengaged war of merely trading intellectual arguments like laser-guided missiles. And our struggle is "not against [people of] flesh and blood". Behind the false religious deceivers and persecutors of the church (who, like Peter, may even be unaware friends—Mark 8:33), there are different kinds of evil power, enslaved by Satan in his wicked objective of opposing God. Satan is trying to keep unbelievers under the tyranny of his lies. His forces are demonic intelligences which may use religions or political ideologies or physical afflictions of many kinds. For instance with Job, the murdering thieves, the fatal storm that killed his servants and children, the skin disease that tortured him and the false teaching of his friends were all employed by Satan. God allowed this suffering because what Satan hoped would tempt Job to doubt, God used to strengthen Job's faith. For Satan's goal is not just the suffering itself—but to use suffering to get God's people to abandon faith in the goodness of God. That is why Christ and his followers are not freed from suffering, but learn to remain faithful in obedience to God in the midst of suffering (Hebrews 5:8).

The important thing for every church and every Christian to recognise is that behind troublesome false teachers are serious demonic powers. This helps us avoid both being cruel towards a person who is deceived (they don't realise that Satan is misleading them) and being naive about nice people who teach falsehood (we mustn't underestimate the damage that Satan will do with his lies, which undermine the gospel). There is a war on—but Christians can be assured that we're on the winning side.

A familiar illustration is helpful here: the successful D-Day landing of Allied forces in France on 6th June 1944 was the decisive victory that ensured victory on the Western Front in World War II, although the Allied troops had to keep fighting the Germans all the way to Berlin until they surrendered on 5th May 1945. In the interim period, the battle was fierce, but ultimate victory was no longer in doubt. Likewise, Christ decisively defeated Satan on the cross but will not destroy him until he returns in judgment. Until then, our struggle with Satan's forces will remain fierce, but our ultimate victory is never in doubt, because of the cross.

> There is a war on—but we're on the winning side.

Paul will now equip us for this struggle by drawing upon the teaching of the prophet Isaiah—about God being the warrior Lord of Hosts, who in Christ has conquered Satan in the armour of his faith in the gospel. Paul begins by locating the source of the strength we will need.

How to be Strong

"Be strong" (Ephesians **6:10**) is literally "be strengthened"—in the mighty power of God. Christ's resurrection power is available to us by his Spirit in our inner being, and he is "able to do immeasurably more than all we ask or imagine, according to his power that is at work within us" (3:20; see also 1:19; 3:16). No situation is beyond God's power to keep us alive in the gospel, and together in world mission, under Christ. Paul's words echo God's triple command to Joshua in leading Israel to occupy Canaan for the LORD: "Be strong and courageous" (Joshua 1:6-9). Joshua's courage foreshadowed the courage of Jesus (whose name is literally "Joshua"), who is leading us to take possession of the whole world for Christ with the gospel. His courageous strength, which preserved his faith in the gospel even unto death, strengthens our faith when we meditate upon him in Scripture and ask him for his strength in prayer.

In this way, our faith in the gospel will be strengthened by Jesus' faith in the gospel—which Paul now likens to wearing the armour of God (Ephesians **6:11**) and is another way to say: "Put on the new self, created to be like God in righteousness and holiness" (4:24).

Questions for reflection

1. How has your view of what "spiritual warfare" is changed as a result of reading this?

2. Do you tend to make too little or too much of the devil and his aims and power? What effect does this have on your view of life and your fight against sin?

3. Are you more likely to be cruel and unloving towards those through whom Satan is working; or naive towards them? How can you remain both loving and wise towards those who mock the church or teach falsehood to the church?

PART TWO

So what is our strategy for surviving Satan's assaults?

Stand Firm!

"Therefore put on the full armour of God, so that when the day of evil comes, you may be able to stand your ground, and after you have done everything, to stand. Stand firm then…" (**6:13-14**). Paul repeats the need to have made preparations for battle by putting on the full armour of God, in order to stand firm against the attack upon our faith by evil powers.

"When the day of evil comes" speaks of the evil days in which we now live, the "last days" before Christ comes; and also of those specific occasions in our lives when Satan is particularly attacking our faith in the gospel that unites our church. The battleground of spiritual warfare will be everyday life—the devil will try to stir up doubts in our minds and divisions in our churches, by undermining our confidence in the mystery of the gospel that unites us. Our goal is to survive, to hold our ground, standing firm together in gospel convictions.

To stand firm to the end is to win in the way that Eleazar, one of King David's mighty men, did, when, as the rest of the Israelite army fled from the Philistine hordes, he "stood his ground and struck down the Philistines till his hand grew tired and froze to the sword. The LORD brought about a great victory that day" (2 Samuel 23:10). And Peter writes: "Your enemy the devil prowls around like a roaring lion looking for someone to devour. Resist him, standing firm in the faith, because you know that the family of believers throughout the world is undergoing the same kind of sufferings" (1 Peter 5:8-9). Spiritual victory is not being freed from suffering, but maintaining faith in the gospel despite it. We too can stand firm in faith if we wear the armour we have been given.

The Full Armour of God

Contrary to what we might expect, when we look carefully at these pieces of armour in Ephesians **6:14-17**, we soon realise that truth, righteousness, peace, faith, salvation and the word of God are not virtuous actions that we are to start doing! Paul is not urging us to be good. Rather, they are all ways of describing the impact of the gospel. The full armour of God, which our champion and commander, Jesus, wore into battle with Satan, is simply faith in the gospel, which the devil wants us to abandon.

The armour of God that Jesus wore is illustrated here with the complete kit of a heavily-armed Roman foot soldier, which Paul amplifies with Isaiah's description of the LORD as a warrior. It is important to recognise that since Christ defeated the devil on the cross, we are not embarking upon a new campaign to attack the devil, but standing still in Christ's victory. We will not be saved by starting new battles with Satan, but by living in confident faith that Christ conquered Satan on the cross. Wearing the armour is not about becoming like Christ enough to defeat Satan, but about staying safe in his finished triumph. We put on the armour of gospel convictions when we first become Christians. Paul is urging his readers to stand firm in that same gospel faith. There's no need to fear Satan while we remain dressed in this armour, because Jesus used it, and has risen from the dead to glory in heaven, which proves that it's effective.

Our spiritual protection against Satan is actually not to worry about him, because we are convinced that he was defeated by the death of Jesus! If we want to be protected from the assaults of the devil, who is trying to force us to abandon our faith, we must simply keep wearing the armour of God that Jesus wore—which is faith in the gospel! Let us look at each piece of armour in turn:

- ■ "The belt of truth buckled round your waist" (**v 14**). Isaiah promised a saviour for whom "righteousness will be his belt and faithfulness the sash round his waist" (Isaiah 11:5). This Saviour is Jesus, who was righteous and faithful. We are wearing the belt of truth when, like a Roman soldier wearing a protective apron or belt, we keep trusting the truth of the gospel that Jesus lived in righteousness and faithfulness for our salvation.

■ "The breastplate of righteousness" (Ephesians **6:14**). Isaiah promised a saviour who would "put on righteousness as his breastplate" (Isaiah 59:17). This is Jesus, who lived a life of perfect righteousness for us. We are wearing this breastplate of righteousness when we keep trusting the gospel that Jesus' righteousness is what qualifies us for heaven and protects us from Satan's condemnation of us under God's law.

■ "Your feet fitted with the readiness that comes from the gospel of peace" (Ephesians **6:15**). Isaiah had promised: "How beautiful on the mountains are the feet of those who bring good news" (Isaiah 52:7). Jesus was the most beautiful evangelist, who "came and preached peace to you who were far away and peace to those who were near" (Ephesians 2:17). We are wearing his sandals of peace when, like troops prepared for battle, we are so trusting in the peace that Jesus secured for us on the cross that we are ready to proclaim it to others.

■ "The shield of faith, with which you can extinguish all the flaming arrows of the evil one" (**6:16**). Proverbs 30:5 promises: "[God] is a shield to those who take refuge in him". And by faith, Jesus took refuge in his Father. We are taking up this shield of faith when, like Roman soldiers protected by full-length shields from arrows tipped with flaming pitch, we are trusting the gospel of Jesus to shield us from Satan's lies.

■ "The helmet of salvation" (Ephesians **6:17**). Isaiah promised a saviour who would wear "the helmet of salvation on his head; he put on the garments of vengeance and wrapped himself in zeal as in a cloak" (Isaiah 59:17). Jesus is this Saviour. And like troops protected by bronze helmets, we are taking the helmet of salvation when we are trusting that Jesus is *our* Saviour and Judge.

■ "The sword of the Spirit, which is the word of God" (Ephesians **6:17**). Isaiah promised a servant who would say: "[The LORD] made my mouth like a sharpened sword" (Isaiah 49:2). Jesus is this servant who wielded the sword of the Spirit, the word of God—which is the only offensive weapon necessary. He defeated the devil in the desert and on the cross by enduring in his faith in the word of the gospel (Matthew 4:1-11). We are like Roman soldiers, wielding short-handled stabbing swords, when we trust in the word that guarantees our salvation. The original Greek word used here is not *logos* (word) but *rhema* (message), which emphasises that the believer is protected not just by understanding the word of the gospel intellectually, but by proclaiming the message of the gospel in response to the temptations, doubts and divisions Satan launches at them.

So, to put on the full armour of God is to resist the lies of Satan with our gospel convictions about the person, life, death, resurrection and reign of Jesus Christ.

While writing these words (in April 2015), I received the all-too familiar news of 147 Christians, mainly students, killed by Islamic extremists in Garissa province, Kenya, a place I visited recently. Their humble and courageous archbishop, Eliud Wabukala, responded with these fine words of gospel confidence:

"We will never surrender our nation or our faith in Christ to those who glory in death and destruction. We will not be intimidated because we know and trust in the power of the cross."

That is exactly what it means to put on the armour of God. While we are wearing this spiritual armour of faith in the gospel, Satan will continually fail in his attempts to stop our churches from demonstrating the wisdom of God in his gathering us under Christ's rule. To be victorious in spiritual warfare, all we have to do is keep trusting the gospel!

Having identified our strength in God, analysed the threat of the enemy to launch his lies at us to create doubts and divisions, clarified our plan to stand firm, and explained the defensive armour of faith in the gospel, Paul now outlines his strategy for victory...

Praying in the Spirit

And that strategy is praying for world mission: "Pray in the Spirit" (Ephesians **6:18**). Prayer is given more attention than any one piece of armour because it's foundational to the effectiveness of all the armour. The importance of prayer for spiritual survival is expressed with the four "alls" of **verse 18**—"on all occasions, with all kinds of prayers", "with all perseverance" (ESV), "for all the Lord's people". This is because we need constantly to pray in our deployment of all the armour of God in our spiritual struggle with evil. If we pray, we'll be safe—and if we don't, we'll be troubled by doubts and divisions. We don't need a complicated battle strategy—we just need a simple commitment to prayer.

Praying "in the Spirit" is not becoming engulfed by ecstatic feelings, but being empowered by the Spirit to pray in accordance with the truth of the Spirit in the gospel of the Bible. For being "filled with the Spirit" (5:18) is accomplished by allowing the word of Christ to "dwell ... richly" in us (Colossians 3:16, ESV). The way in which we let the Bible "dwell richly" in us is to surrender ourselves to meditate upon the word until we believe it. So with the Holy Spirit's help, let us pray...

- "On all occasions" (Ephesians **6:18**), especially when doubts threaten to damage our confidence in Christ or when tensions arise to threaten our church unity.

- "With all kinds of prayers and requests", whether in urgent and spontaneous **"arrow" prayers**, short prayers at the beginning and end of each every church meeting, set prayers and *extempore* prayers during church, praying personally at the beginning and end of our normal day, or praying for longer periods at times of pressure and decision. And, especially, in regularly praying the prayer Jesus told us to (Matthew 6:9-13), which so brilliantly summarises gospel priorities.

■ "Keep on praying for all the Lord's people" (Ephesians **6:18**). We are to keep praying for each other. We may feel powerless to help God's people around the world, especially those who are suffering persecution for him, but God loves the prayers of those who are moved to pray for his family. However weak or inexperienced we may feel, we can all pray for unity in the gospel for our church and all the families and businesses represented in it, praying for them to the One who is with them. This vital but under-appreciated ministry of prayer is something in which those who are older and less active but who may have more time available can excel.

And Paul shows that what we especially need to pray for each other is to be courageous in our evangelism: "Pray also for me, that whenever I speak, words may be given me so that I will fearlessly make known the mystery of the gospel, for which I am an ambassador in chains. Pray that I may declare it fearlessly, as I should" (**v 19-20**).

> God loves the prayers of those who are moved to pray for his family.

Paul twice asks for prayer to preach "fearlessly". The reason is clear from his reference to the "mystery of the gospel", which we know from chapter 3 is the revelation that Jew and Gentile, and people from all nations alike, can and must be saved through faith in Christ crucified. It was this message that brought him persecution from zealous Jewish leaders, and is the reason for his current imprisonment "in chains".

Jesus said to his followers that "if they persecuted me, they will persecute you also" (John 15:20). Paul wrote: "In fact, everyone who wants to live a godly life in Christ Jesus will be persecuted" (2 Timothy 3:12). Dietrich Bonhoeffer, the German pastor imprisoned and finally executed for his opposition to Hitler's Nazism, wrote from his prison:

"The cross is laid on every Christian. When Christ calls a man, he bids him come and die ... Suffering then, is the badge of true discipleship. The disciple is not above his master ... if we refuse to take up our cross and submit to suffering and rejection at the hands of men, we forfeit our fellowship with Christ and have ceased to follow him. But if we lose our lives in his service and carry our cross, we shall find our lives again in the fellowship of the cross with Christ." (*The Cost of Discipleship*, page 80)

So we must all expect to suffer for following Christ—and therefore we need to pray for ourselves and each other, that we will proclaim Christ "fearlessly" (Ephesians **6:19-20**).

In secular Western cultures, it may mean enduring mockery from our friends, pity from our family and aggression on the doorstep. It certainly means enduring the frustrating hypocrisy of our national leaders marching in the cause of free speech—as when the offices of the satirical French magazine *Charlie Hebdo* were shockingly attacked by terrorists—while forbidding Christians nurses and teachers from speaking of Christ, and also largely ignoring the systematic physical and commercial persecution of Christians throughout the world. Of course, for our Christian brothers and sisters watching their loved ones crucified or buried alive by Isil in Iraq, or being used for testing biological weapons or watching their church leaders laid down while a steamroller crushed their skulls in North Korea, it's a lot more than frustrating.

So pray for all who preach; pray for your brothers and sisters in Islamic and totalitarian nations; and pray for everyone in your church—to proclaim the truth of the mystery of the gospel fearlessly. Pray that when they are persecuted, they will see themselves not as disgraced victims but, like Paul, as "ambassadors in chains" (**v 20**), the dignified representatives of their persecuted King.

Satan wants to prevent people from being gathered into the church of Christ and demonstrating his defeat at the cross in the spiritual realms. Paul tells us to stand firm in the gospel and pray for world mission. So spiritual warfare means putting on the full armour of God worn by Christ, which is faith in the gospel being expressed in prayer for evangelism.

Questions for reflection

1. Consider a time recently when you gave in to temptation. What aspect of gospel truth had you failed to remember and live by—ie: to "wear"? How can you stand firm next time that temptation comes?

2. When are you most likely to be "fearful" about speaking out about Christ, and therefore remain quiet? Who will you ask to pray for you?

3. The home and the workplace are battlegrounds in which we are called to stand firm against the devil's schemes. What might that look like for you today? Where will the battle be hardest, and how will you stand?

13. CONCLUSION: FAREWELL WORDS

Paul now briefly concludes this glorious circular letter from prison to the churches of Ephesus. He is sending it with his loyal apprentice, Tychicus, who will encourage them with news (**v 22**). Paul describes him as a "dear brother and faithful servant in the Lord" (**v 21**). The apostle was not in the habit of dispensing exaggerated flattery, but it is surely the highest of accolades for any believer to be commended by Christ's apostle as "faithful" to the Lord. Indeed, this is the praise that we are all to invest our efforts and resources in; that, having stood firm by faith in the gospel, Christ might welcome us into his kingdom with the words: "Well done, good and faithful servant" (Matthew 25:21, 23). The measure of our lives and ministries is not the size of our salary, or the number of our grandchildren, or the turnover of our business, or the size of our church, but whether we have proved faithful in believing and proclaiming the mystery of the gospel for all nations, even when it hurts.

Paul's farewell words deliberately emphasise the three major blessings of God in Christ that are prominent throughout this letter (as well as his others). He signs off with the result, the content and the origin of God's glorious plan to unite everything under Christ.

The first farewell blessing is "peace" (Ephesians **6:23**). This was the customary word of Jewish greeting (*shalom*), but here it signifies more than happiness—it is the wonderful reconciliation with God and with each other for which Christ died, by which we are gathered together under Christ in his church. Indeed Christ "is our peace"—the One in whom we are united, because he died, "thus making peace" by satisfying God for our sins, so that "he came and preached peace" (2:14-17). Peace well summarises the eternal blessing of salvation in Christ, which results from the mystery of the gospel.

The second farewell blessing is "love" (**6:23**). God's eternal plan not only reveals how impressive he is, but how compassionate he is; not just how powerful he is, but how loving. Paul has already celebrated how immense this love for us is (3:18)—a "wide" and accepting love that saves sinners from every nation (2:19); a "long" and lasting love that predestined us from before creation in the past, and preserves us for resurrection into an eternal future (1:4-5; 2:7); a "high" and exalting love that has raised us to glory in the heavenly realms, where he will shower us with the riches of his grace (2:6); and a "deep" and sacrificial love, so rich in sacrificial mercy that he made us alive with Christ (2:4-5). Love well summarises the substance of what we experience in Christ through faith in the mystery of the gospel.

> God's plan reveals not just how impressive he is, but how compassionate.

And finally, the third farewell blessing is God's "grace" (**6:24**). This undeserved and extravagant kindness is the origin of God's plan not only to gather us into his church to display his wisdom in the spiritual realms, but "in order that in the coming ages he might show the incomparable riches of his grace, expressed in his kindness to us in Christ Jesus" (2:7). Grace is the origin of the mystery of the gospel, now revealed in Christ to all who continue to love him with "an undying love" (**6:24**) empowered by his resurrection. Since our salvation comes entirely from his grace, all glory in the church must be given entirely and eternally to him. Let that be so of our churches and our lives.

Questions for reflection

1. How has Ephesians given you a greater appreciation of gospel peace, gospel love, and gospel grace?

2. How has Ephesians equipped you to serve God by serving his church?

3. What practical change to the way you live has the Spirit been calling you to as you have enjoyed the great truths of this letter?

GLOSSARY

Abraham: (also called Abram) the ancestor of the nation of Israel, and the man God made a binding agreement (covenant) with. God promised to make his family into a great nation, give them a land, and bring blessing to all nations through one of his descendants (see Genesis 12:1-3).

Analogy: a comparison between two things, usually using one of them to explain or clarify the other.

Anglican 39 Articles of Faith: a statement of what the Church of England believed, drawn up in 1563.

Annihilation: destruction; ceasing to exist.

Apostle: a man appointed directly by the risen Christ to teach about him with his authority.

Arius: a church leader in Egypt in the third century. Taught (wrongly) that God the Son is not eternal, but was created by God the Father.

Arminians: those who do not believe in predestination, holding that God desires to save everyone, and that humans decide whether to respond to his offer of grace, so that salvation depends on human decision, not God's initiative.

Arrow prayers: short prayers "fired up" to God in the midst of everyday life.

Ascetics: those who refrain from fun and pleasure for religious reasons.

Athanasius: bishop of Alexandria (Egypt) in the third century. Defended the biblical truth that God the Son has always existed, and is fully God.

Atonement: a way of coming back into relationship with someone.

Augustine: a 4th-century bishop in north Africa (modern-day Algeria) He taught that sin has entirely corrupted our human nature, and that we are powerless to overcome it, and so salvation is entirely God's gift and initiative.

Autonomy: the ability to make our own decisions without being directed by anyone else; to be self-governing.

Calvary: the place on the outskirts of Jerusalem where Jesus was crucified.

Calvin, John: a French theologian and pastor during the Reformation in the 16th century, based mainly in Geneva. Among other things, he taught that God chooses whom he will save—humans do not decide for themselves.

Circumcision: God told the men among his people in the Old Testament to be circumcised as a way to show physically that they knew and trusted him, and belonged to the people of God (see Genesis 17).

Commandment: here, referring to the 10 Commandments given by God to Moses on Mount Sinai (see Exodus 20:1-17)

Concurrent: happening at the same time.

Conversion: the moment when someone for the first time recognises Jesus, God's Son, as Lord, and turns to him as Saviour.

Covenant: a binding agreement between two parties.

Digression: a side-note, having temporarily left the main subject.

Dominion: control.

Epistle: letter.

Ethics: a set of moral principles.

Evangelise, evangelism: to tell non-Christians the gospel of Jesus Christ. An **evangelist** is a person who does this and equips other Christians to do it.

Exorcisms: casting an evil spirit from a person who appears to be possessed.

Experientially: in real-life experience.

Extempore: spoken without preparation.

Ezra: priest during the time when Jews returned from exile in Babylon to Jerusalem.

Galilean: someone from the region of Galilee, in the north of first-century Israel.

Hedonism: the pursuit of pleasure.

Hierarchy: where people are ranked in order of importance or status.

Homogeneous: where things are of the same kind; alike.

Jordan: a river; the Jordan river was the eastern border of Canaan. The Israelites had to cross it before they could enter the promised land.

Joshua: leader of the people of Israel after Moses. One of only two people who were both rescued from slavery in Egypt *and* also set foot in the promised land of Canaan. This is a different Joshua to the high priest of the same name who served during the prophet Zechariah's time.

Justification: the declaration that someone is not guilty, not condemned, completely innocent.

Lay: voluntary; not ordained or formally trained.

Liberal: professing Christians who do not view Scripture as without error.

Luther: Martin Luther, a German theologian in the 16th century during the Reformation. Taught that humans are made right with God through faith in Christ, not through what we do.

Masochistic: enjoying what is painful.

Mass: the Roman Catholic service of holy communion.

Mediate: act as a go-between for two parties in a dispute.

Meditate: focus one's mind on.

Metaphors: images which are used to explain something, but that are not to be taken literally (eg: "The news was a dagger to his heart").

Moses: the leader of God's people at the time when God brought them out of slavery in Egypt. God communicated his law (including the Ten Commandments) through Moses, and under Moses' leadership God guided them toward the land he had promised to give them.

Nehemiah: a Jewish official in the Persian court, who oversaw the return of a group of Israelites to Jerusalem after their exile in Babylon, and the rebuilding of the city's walls.

Occult: magical practices often drawing on sinister supernatural powers.

Open theologians: argue that God's plan for the future is "open" as opposed to being fixed: he has a number of possibilities, and human will determines what actually happens.

Pagan: someone who doesn't know and worship the true God.

Pelagius: a British-born thinker in the early 5th century. Believed that humans are able to fulfil God's law by their own effort without God's help, because they are not innately sinful.

Plural: more than one; here, referring to the fact that God is a Trinity of Father, Son and Holy Spirit.

Purgatory: in Roman Catholic thought, the place where the souls of the dead are believed to go to be "purged" of their sin, before they are fit to enter heaven.

Rationalistic: the idea that our beliefs about the world around us should be based on reason and scientific knowledge, not emotions or experience (or, indeed, Scripture).

Reformed theologians / Reformer: one of the first two generations of people in the fifteenth and early-sixteenth centuries who preached the gospel of justification by faith, and opposed the Pope and the Roman church.

Sacraments: in the Protestant church, the Lord's Supper (communion) and baptism are considered sacraments. Other denominations hold that there are more, and other, "sacraments" (eg: Roman Catholic "mass").

Saints: Christians.

Samuel: a prophet who led Israel before King Saul.

Sanctified: made pure; changed to become like Christ (see Romans 8:29).

Saul: the first king of Israel (see 1 Samuel 8 – 10).

Secular atheism: the belief that God does not exist—so human society, governments, etc should be run completely separately from any religious beliefs.

Social evolution: the idea that social practices and customs have developed over human history as a survival mechanism.

Sovereignty: supreme authority / being the supreme ruler.

Tabernacled: when the Israelites lived in the wilderness, the tabernacle was a large, tented area where the Israelites worshipped God, and where his presence symbolically dwelled (see Exodus 26; 40). In John 1:14, the writer uses the same word to describe how God's Son "made his dwelling" among humans.

The grim reaper: death, personified as a cloaked skeleton holding a large scythe.

Theologians: those who study theology—the study of the truth about God.

Trajectories: paths, courses or patterns.

Transgressions: sins. Literally, the word means "stepped across a line".

Trinity: the biblical doctrine that the one God is three Persons, distinct from one another, each fully God, of the same "essence" (or "Godness"). We usually call these three Persons Father, Son and Holy Spirit. **Triune** is a word which is used to describe this aspect of God's nature.

Wrath: God's settled, justified hatred of and anger at sin.

Zion: another name for Jerusalem (more specifically, the mountain upon which it was built).

APPENDIX: A Summary of Ephesians

The letter neatly divides into two halves of three chapters, each chapter conveniently diving in two:

Chapters 1 – 3: Gospel doctrine

Paul proclaims God's cosmic plan to unite everything under Christ (1:10), by reconciling us to God and each other by his death and resurrection (2:4-6, 14), through the proclamation of the revealed mystery of the gospel of Christ crucified for all nations, that is displayed in his church to the spiritual realms (3:6, 10).

1:1-14:　is an explosion of praise to God for every spiritual blessing in the spiritual realms in Christ; supreme among them is being chosen for adoption by the Father, redeemed for revelation by the Son and sealed for inheritance by the Spirit—in which God's focus is summing up all things in the heavenly realms and on earth in Christ.

1:15-23:　is a report of Paul's prayers for his readers to experience the precious spiritual privileges of knowing God better, knowing the hope to which he's called us, and knowing the resurrection power which he has committed to bringing us to be with him.

2:1-10:　is a celebration of God's amazing grace in bringing us from being dead in sin by nature, to life by grace in Christ—this is in order that in the coming ages he might show us the incomparable riches of his grace.

2:11-22:　proclaims that believing Gentiles, previously separated, excluded, and foreign to the blessings of Israel, have been reconciled with believing Jews in a new humanity in Christ, through his death that destroyed the barrier of the law; so now people of all nations may become citizens of God's kingdom and members of his family, built upon the gospel of Christ and growing as the holy temple dwelling of God.

3:1-13:   explains that Paul's imprisonment for preaching Christ cru-
           cified was all part of God's glorious plan to use despised
           messengers to advertise the mystery of the gospel, now re-
           vealed, that people of all nations can share in the blessings
           of Christ; this is so that the wisdom of God in the gospel of
           Christ crucified might be displayed to the evil powers in the
           spiritual realms in the trophy cabinet of his church.

3:14-21:   reveals Paul's prayers for God to grant his readers power
           to become holy people, fit dwellings for the presence of
           God's Spirit; and for power to appreciate how wide and ac-
           cepting, long and lasting, high and exalting and deep and
           sacrificial is the massive love of Christ for us; to him be all
           the glory!

Chapters 4 – 6: The practice of gospel churches

Paul calls upon churches to respond to the truths of the first three
chapters by preserving their unity under Christ—preparing each other
for ministry to grow in maturity by speaking the truth in love, in order to be made new in their minds, live Christ-honouring lives in the
church, at home and at work, and stand firm in the gospel against the
devil's schemes.

4:1-16:   calls the readers to live lives worthy of our calling by apply-
           ing our spiritual unity in Christ to a practical unity in church;
           this can be done through Bible-teaching that equips church
           members to contribute their ministry to grow the church in
           maturity into Christ.

4:17-32:   calls the readers to preserve their unity by putting off the
           worldly thinking of our old selves and to be renewed with
           godly minds of Christ-like love; Paul gives practical exam-
           ples of loving attitudes and speech to become imitators of
           God by living lives of love, just as Christ loved us.

5:1-20:   calls the readers to preserve their unity by living as chil-
           dren of light by abstaining from immorality, impurity and

greed; Paul calls them instead to be filled with the Holy Spirit, speaking to each other and to God with songs of thanksgiving.

5:21-33: begins a section on the unity of household relationships in the church by calling on wives to submit to their husbands in everything as the church submits to Christ; and upon husbands to love their wives sacrificially as Christ has loved the church and as a person loves their own body; Paul concludes by explaining that this discussion of marriage is really about the gospel mystery of the intimate union of Christ with his church.

6:1-9: calls the readers to peace in serving Christ at home and at work—telling children to honour their parents and fathers not to frustrate their children, but to raise them in the instruction of the Lord; and telling slaves (and employees) to serve wholeheartedly as to the Lord, and masters to treat their workers well as they share the same master in heaven.

6:10-23: is the climactic finale of the letter calling readers to stand firm against the lies of Satan that will threaten to divide them from God and from each other; they will be strengthened by God to stand firm in the armour of God worn by Christ in defeating Satan at the cross, ie: gospel convictions; and to keep on praying for world mission—this is victory in spiritual warfare.

BIBLIOGRAPHY

- Dietrich Bonhoeffer, *The Cost of Discipleship* (SCM, 1990)

- F.F. Bruce, *The Epistles to the Colossians, to Philemon, and to the Ephesians* in the New International Commentary on the New Testament series (Eerdmans, 2nd ed, 1984)

- John Bunyan, *Praying with the Spirit and with Understanding Too* (1663)

- Gary Chapman, *The Five Love Languages* (Northfield, 2004)

- Richard Dawkins, *The God Delusion* (Black Swan, 2007)

- William Hendriksen, *Exposition of Galatians, Ephesians, Philippians, Colossians, and Philemon* in the New Testament Commentary series (Baker Academic, 1996)

- Charles Hodge, *Ephesians* in the Geneva Series of Commentaries (Banner of Truth, 1964)

- H.A. Ironside, *In the Heavenlies: Practical Expository Addresses on the Epistle to the Ephesians* (Loizeaux Brothers, 1937)

- C.S. Lewis, *Mere Christianity* (MacMillan, 1960)

- Andrew T. Lincoln et al, *Ephesians* in the Word Biblical Commentary series (Zondervan, 2014)

- Peter T. O'Brien, *The Letter to the Ephesians* in the Pillar New Testament Commentary series (Eerdmans, 1999)

- J.I. Packer, *Knowing God* (Hodder & Stoughton, 1975)

- J.C. Ryle, *Heaven* (Christian Focus, 1991)

- C.H. Spurgeon, *The Immutability of God* (available online at: spurgeon.org/sermons.0001.htm)

- John Stott, *The Message of Ephesians* in the Bible Speaks Today series (IVP/IVP Academic, 1984)

- David F. Wells, *Losing our Virtue* (Eerdmans, 1999)

More For You

1 Samuel For You

"As we read this gripping part of Israel's history, we see Jesus Christ with fresh colour and texture. And we see what it means for his people to follow him as King in an age that worships personal freedom."

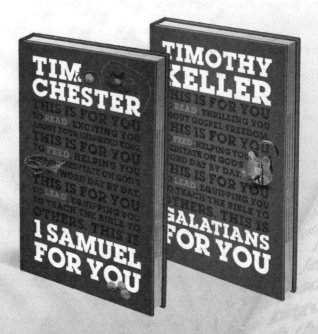

Galatians For You

"The book of Galatians is dynamite. It is an explosion of joy and freedom which leaves us enjoying a deep significance, security and satisfaction. Why? Because it brings us face to face with the gospel—the A to Z of the Christian life."

The Series

Other titles in the *God's Word For You* series are:

- **Exodus For You** *Tim Chester*
- **Judges For You** *Timothy Keller*
- **1 Samuel For You** *Tim Chester*
- **Daniel For You** *David Helm*
- **Luke 1-12 For You** *Mike McKinley*
- **Luke 12-24 For You** *Mike McKinley*
- **John 1-12 For You** *Josh Moody*
- **Romans 1-7 For You** *Timothy Keller*
- **Romans 8-16 For You** *Timothy Keller*
- **Galatians For You** *Timothy Keller*
- **Philippians For You** *Steven Lawson*
- **Titus For You** *Tim Chester*
- **James For You** *Sam Allberry*
- **1 Peter For You** *Juan Sanchez*

Forthcoming titles include:

- **Micah For You** *Stephen Um*
- **Acts For You (two volumes)**
  Albert Mohler
- **1, 2 & 3 John For You** *H.B. Charles, Jr.*
- **Revelation For You** *Tim Chester*

Find out more about these resources at:

www.thegoodbook.com/for-you

thegoodbook
COMPANY

BIBLICAL | RELEVANT | ACCESSIBLE

At The Good Book Company, we are dedicated to helping Christians and local churches grow. We believe that God's growth process always starts with hearing clearly what he has said to us through his timeless word—the Bible.

Ever since we opened our doors in 1991, we have been striving to produce resources that honour God in the way the Bible is used. We have grown to become an international provider of user-friendly resources to the Christian community, with believers of all backgrounds and denominations using our Bible studies, books, evangelistic resources, DVD-based courses and training events.

We want to equip ordinary Christians to live for Christ day by day, and churches to grow in their knowledge of God, their love for one another, and the effectiveness of their outreach.

Call us for a discussion of your needs or visit one of our local websites for more information on the resources and services we provide.

Your friends at The Good Book Company

UK & EUROPE
NORTH AMERICA
AUSTRALIA
NEW ZEALAND

thegoodbook.co.uk
thegoodbook.com
thegoodbook.com.au
thegoodbook.co.nz

0333 123 0880
866 244 2165
(02) 9564 3555
(+64) 3 343 2463

WWW.CHRISTIANITYEXPLORED.ORG
Our partner site is a great place for those exploring the Christian faith, with a clear explanation of the good news, powerful testimonies and answers to difficult questions.